THE
25
RULES
OF
GRAMMAR

By the same author:

The Story of English
This Book Will Make You Think
(as Alain Stephen)
Symbols

THE
25
RULES

—— OF ——

GRAMMAR

The Essential Guide to
Good English

JOSEPH PIERCY

Michael O'Mara Books Limited

First published in Great Britain in 2014 by
Michael O'Mara Books Limited
9 Lion Yard
Tremadoc Road
London SW4 7NQ

A CIP catalogue record for this book is available from the British
Library.

Papers used by Michael O'Mara Books Limited are natural, recyclable
products made from wood grown in sustainable forests. The
manufacturing processes conform to the environmental regulations of
the country of origin.

ISBN: 978-1-78243-231-9 in hardback print format
ISBN: 978-1-78243-268-5 in e-book format

1 2 3 4 5 6 7 8 9 10

Cover design by Ana Bježančević
Designed and typeset by K. DESIGN, Winscombe, Somerset

Printed and bound by CPI Group (UK) Ltd, Croydon, CR0 4YY

www.mombooks.com

This book is dedicated to my friend Rainer.
If he *were* alive he would *be* amused.

Rainer Lange
(1964–2008)

Contents

'Who climbs the grammar tree, distinctly knows
Where noun, and verb, and participle grows.'

John Dryden
(1631–1700)

Acknowledgements

My heartfelt thanks to the following people for their kindness, patience and fortitude in the creation of this book:

Firstly to Louise Dixon for getting the project off the ground in the first place and her kindly advice and encouragement, and Gabriella Nemeth, an absolute dream of an editor – skilful, diplomatic, and in possession of almost limitless resources of patience. I'd also like to thank the staff at Sussex University Library and Hove Library; R. Lucas and James Fleet and most of all my family and friends for putting up with my tiresome pedantry about all things grammar, particularly Joanna and my daughter Polly. I have dedicated this book to my friend Rainer Lange, a German national who loved to correct the English on their English.

Introduction

Does Grammar Really Matter?

Yes. It does. Matter. Because how, wood you under stand; what I is saying?

My personal experience of grammar lessons at school was, at best pretty torpid and, at worst downright arduous. This scale encouraged neither interest or learning. I only really became very totally interested in grammar when training to become an EFL teacher. Although English hadn't not become my subject; I'd flirted with being an artist (couldn't draw) and a musician (couldn't play an instrument) and I liked reading books. Lots of books. You can never have enough books. And real books too!

Eagle-eyed grammarians would argue that the last sentence of the previous paragraph isn't a sentence. And they wouldn't not be right. After a fashion. But I am better now than I were before . . .

Shall I start again?

Does grammar really matter? Well, I have tried to break as many grammatical rules in the opening to this introduction as possible to see if anybody notices. It is a *Where's Wally?* of grammar errors but, although it reads a touch like experimental fiction in parts, it is fairly coherent.

The current trends in English grammar fall into two schools. On one side are the 'prescriptivists', the 'Olde School', those who phone in to the BBC to complain about minor errors in news reports on national television and radio. On the other side are the 'descriptivists', the 'New Skool', those who feel that language is always evolving and that therefore grammar should evolve too. Fundamentally, the argument comes down to one sticking point about the nature of how language actually functions. Is usage determined by grammatical rules? Or are grammatical rules defined by usage?

In order to function as a practical means of communication a language needs a vocabulary and a grammar. Every written language in the world has a grammatical structure, rules that govern, determine and define how meaning is produced. This seems more than plausible and, although I started this introduction by trying to deliberately flout (not flaunt) the rules, precision in thought and, by extension, clarity of expression *are* important.

On the other hand, there is a counter-argument that if people keep making the same mistakes, over and over again, after a while it is no longer a mistake but becomes commonplace and therefore correct. It is certainly true that lots of grammatical forms: words, moods and structures, have fallen out of general usage. The use of 'shall', for example, as a future form has been reduced to little more than polite requests or offers ('Shall we go to the pub?'; 'Shall I buy you a drink?') in the last century and a half. Other words such as 'forensic' have taken on a whole new meaning in less than thirty years. 'Forensic' was originally a legal term that had nothing at all to do with cutting up the dead bodies of murder victims; it means simply, the practice of rhetoric associated with legal matters, the presentation of argument supported by evidence in a court of law. On any given day you can turn on the television and a crime drama will talk about the need of getting the 'forensics' in order to achieve an arrest and probable conviction. They only actually need the forensics in court, they don't need them beforehand as it is a matter of rhetoric, not minute skin fibres or complicated DNA test results.

The English language has lots of rules, over 2,000 to be imprecise. Some of these rules are archaic and arguably unnecessary. The first attempts at writing down the essential rules of grammar surfaced in the mid-eighteenth century. Bishop Robert Lowth's *A Short Introduction To English Grammar* (1762) proved extremely popular at the time and unbeknown to the kindly, but somewhat pedantic clergyman, set in motion arguments on correct and incorrect usage that still rage on to this day. Lowth was directly responsible for several of the grammatical shibboleths analysed in this book; some of them still hold true but at least one of them is at best outmoded and at worst, bogus in the first place. The irony concerning Robert Lowth's influence on English grammar is that his book was written as a guide to correct English usage for his son Thomas and was never intended to be published, let alone spark centuries of argument and rancour.

Lowth's rules were taken up by a whole generation of Victorian grammarians, who followed his ideas that you could apply the grammatical rules of Latin to modern English. Unfortunately, this rather spurious premise has caused the entire furore. The Olde School stick to the rules stringently as a badge of status and superiority over the New Skool whom they believe are ill-educated and only semi-literate. The New Skool, with some justification, view their detractors as stuffy, elitist snobs.

The two grammar camps are poles apart and will never be reconciled so perhaps it is time to try and find a third way. In my opinion, the English language is under much less threat from sloppy usage or the influence of modern technology than it is from the language of modern marketing and commerce. The Greek term 'pleonasm' refers to unnecessary words placed next to each other to produce largely redundant phrases. Advertising is full of pleonasms such as 'extra bonus' and 'free gift' or even 'extra bonus free gift' just in case you didn't quite grasp the concept first time round. Knowing and being able to spot such nonsense is a valuable skill and preserving a sense of clarity and quality of expression in written and spoken language is also vital so as to see through all the bilge and balderdash. This, more than anything else, is a viable argument for understanding some of the 'essential rules' and knowing when it is OK to break them. In this view, grammar does matter, for frankly horrible phrases such as 'blue-sky thinking' only stem from cloudy thoughts.

Joseph Piercy
Brighton 2014

The Essential Tools
Building Blocks and Basics

There are nine word classes (also known as parts of speech) in the English language: **nouns**, **pronouns**, **verbs**, **adjectives**, **adverbs**, **prepositions**, **conjunctions**, **interjections** and **articles**, and various sub-categories within the nine classes. Rather than throw all nine in the pot at once, these ingredients need to be handled with care and added a little at a time so each individual part of speech can be measured out according to the rules they relate to. It should be stressed, however, that the function of an individual word and the word class it belongs to depends on where it is positioned in a sentence and hence its relationship to other words.

For example, consider the following three sentences and the meaning of the word *work*:

1. *I was late for **work**.*

2. *I will **work** hard to grasp the essentials of grammar.*

3. *You will need a **work** permit to teach in China.*

In the first sentence, *work* functions as a noun (the place, or thing 'I' am late for); in the second sentence, *work* functions as a verb (the action needed to achieve a stated objective); and in the third sentence, *work* functions as an adjunct noun, a noun that modifies or determines another noun (permit) and therefore performs the same role as an adjective.

In general, sentences in English follow a standard subject, verb, object word order. The subject of a sentence is the person, place, thing, or idea that is *doing* or *being* something. The subject of a sentence can usually be found by identifying the verb and determining who or what it relates to. For example, in the first sentence, *was* is the verb (past tense of *to be*), followed by the adverb of time *late* and the object noun *work*, so *I* is the subject. The object of a sentence therefore follows the verb and is the person, place or thing that the action or state is being directed towards. One note of caution however, is that some sentences do not follow the subject, verb, object order in quite such a straightforward structure. There are several situations where it is common practice for the subject to follow the verb. Question forms are a good example of an inverted word order (verbs in **bold**/subject underlined):

Have <u>you</u> my keys?

In this case the order is verb (*have*), subject (*you*) and object noun (*keys*).

Sentences that begin with an adverb (a word that adds to the meaning of a verb, adjective or even another adverb) or adverbial phrase are other common constructions that follow a different word order, principally to provide emphasis as in Winston Churchill's famous speech:

> *'Never in the field of human conflict was so much owed by so many to so few.'*

The deliberate inversion of the standard word order is used to powerful effect as to rewrite the sentence as 'A debt has never been owed by so many to so few in the field of human conflict' sounds fussy and barely makes any sense (although neither does Churchill's original if you look at it closely).

Inverting word order is also common when used for literary or stylistic effect as in Alfred Lord Tennyson's poem 'The Charge of the Light Brigade' (1854):

> *'Into the valley of death rode the six hundred.'*

In this case the sentence starts with a preposition (*into*) (words that *position* nouns or pronouns in sentences and clauses) followed by the object, the verb and the subject. 'The six hundred rode into the valley of death' adds little tension or excitement, in fact, there isn't much point going on with the story.

The two quotes above are exceptions to standard word order, messed about with for specific purposes of rhetoric and style. In order to keep things simple we need to start with the basics and the most basic unit of language is the sentence.

Rule 1

When is a Sentence Not a Sentence?

The Rule: Sentences must contain a subject and a predicate, express a complete idea, begin with a capital letter and end with appropriate punctuation marks.

The parts of speech are the building blocks used to create grammatical units commonly known as sentences. Think of these word classes in terms of a vast Lego set where the constituent parts can be combined and recombined to create wondrous and great-looking things. However, similar to Lego, not all of the pieces fit comfortably together and need to be attached in the right place and correct sequence in order to achieve their goal. Sentences are often described as containing and expressing a complete idea and this idea can satisfy a variety of different functions. A *declarative* sentence contains statements and observations, such as 'I am a writer.' An *interrogative* sentence, as the name suggests, asks questions and elicits information such as 'Am I a writer?' (this could also be a rhetorical question, of course). Exclamatory questions also contain statements but have added emphasis to express feeling and emotion as in 'I am a writer! I am not a banker!'. The fourth function of sentences is provided by *imperative* sentences containing commands and instructions such as 'I must write!'

In linguistic terms, sentences can be divided into three main classes according to their structure: *simple* sentences, *compound* sentences and *complex* sentences (some grammarians have identified a fourth class, the *compound-complex* sentence but that is just showing off). These classifications are based on the number and type of clauses an individual sentence contains. The traditional definition of a clause is a collection of words that contains a *subject* and a *predicate*. Without wishing to get too bogged down with linguistic terminology regarding what constitutes a *subject* and *predicate*, the simplest explanation is the *subject* is who or what is actively 'doing' something and the *predicate* is everything else. In the sentence 'the dog barks', 'the dog' is the *subject* and 'barks' the *predicate*. The above example is a *simple* sentence in that it contains a single main clause (also called an independent clause) that contains a complete idea. The sentence 'the dog barks, and the cat meows', is a *compound* sentence because it contains two independent clauses linked by a conjunction ('and').

Complex sentences are sentences that contain an independent clause and a secondary dependent clause (also called a subordinate clause). Dependent clauses, as the name suggests, depend on the main (independent) clause in order to make sense. Dependent clauses provide additional information that can modify the main clause or act as a constituent part. For example:

The dog barks because it is hungry, but the cat meows because it is tired, or when it wants to be stroked.

The sentence above contains two independent clauses (as identified previously) plus three subordinate clauses (*because it is hungry/tired/when it wants to be stroked*) so strictly speaking it is what is known as a *compound-complex* sentence but personally I have an issue with fussy terminology and besides, something is either simple or it's complex, let's not overcomplicate the complex.

So that, in essence, is how to identify what constitutes a sentence, the function or purpose it satisfies and its constituent parts, but doesn't fully explain what isn't a sentence.

As stated earlier, a sentence, in order to be a sentence, must contain a subject and a predicate (a verb and quite often an object) and most importantly must express a complete idea and function in the form of a main or independent clause, and start with a capital letter and end with a full stop, question or exclamation mark. Consider the 'sentences' below:

1. *In Britain, after The Great War and before the outbreak of hostilities in 1945.*

2. *Many **students reading** about grammar in the local library.*

3. *Although **she was** by far the better writer and **had** an excellent felicity with words.*

At first glance, sentences one to three seem to be complete sentences in that they make sense and express ideas. They are however, what is known as *sentence fragments* and on closer inspection there seems to be something not quite right about them. Sentence one, although containing a good deal of subject material and context (time/place) doesn't actually contain a subject or a verb and so can't be a complete sentence. Sentence two qualifies as a fragment for although it appears to have a subject (*students*) and a verb (*reading*); the verb is actually a dangling present participle and doesn't have an auxiliary verb preceding it so therefore isn't actually a verb at all. 'Many students **were reading** about grammar in the local library' is a complete sentence. Sentence three is a sentence fragment that seems to throw our rule out of the window as it contains a subject (*she*) and two verbs (*was* and *had*) but the problem here is that the sentence contains the word 'although', which is what is known in grammatical terms as a 'subordinating conjunction'. The word 'although' modifies the clause, making it a dependent clause (or subordinate clause) that requires an independent or main clause to make sense:

*Although she was by far the better writer and had an
excellent felicity with words, the judges gave the literary
prize to somebody else instead.*

Is Too Much Better Than Not Enough?

The ability to handle multiple subordinate clauses skilfully
is considered to be the signature of fine writing. There are
dangers and pitfalls in getting carried away by linking too
many ideas together in the same sentence. The result is that
even the most attentive reader will find the writer's train
of thought difficult to follow. Below are two examples
from classics of English literature that at first glance are
bewilderingly long sentences:

> *'He got a good estate by merchandise, and leaving
> off his trade, lived afterwards at York, from
> whence he had married my mother, whose relations
> were named Robinson, a very good family in that
> country, and from whom I was called Robinson
> Kreutznaer; but, by the usual corruption of words
> in England, we are now called – nay we call
> ourselves and write our name – Crusoe; and so my
> companions always called me.'*

> *The Adventures of Robinson Crusoe*
> Daniel Defoe

> *'This great man, as is well known to all lovers of*
> *polite eating, begins at first by setting plain things*
> *before his hungry guests, rising afterwards by degrees*
> *as their stomachs may be supposed to decrease, to the*
> *very quintessence of sauce and spices.'*

The Adventures of Tom Jones
Henry Fielding

Conversely, short, sharp staccato sentences can be equally perplexing as the opening to Charles Dickens' *Bleak House* demonstrates:

> *'London. Michaelmas term lately over, and the*
> *Lord Chancellor sitting in Lincoln's Inn Hall.*
> *Implacable November weather.'*

Dickens demonstrates three very different forms of sentences in this brief passage, none of which contain a finite verb (*sitting* being a present participle). The great man just about gets away with it though under the rule that a sentence is an idea contained within a capital letter and a full stop, and just to show he can do other types of sentence as well the passage continues with some delightful subordinate clauses, especially the giant lizard, which is such a terrific image he mentions it twice (see Rule 15):

'As much mud in the streets as if the waters had but newly retired from the face of the earth, and it would not be wonderful to meet a Megalosaurus, forty feet long or so, waddling like an elephantine lizard up Holborn Hill.'

Bleak House
Charles Dickens

In Summary

As the examples we have seen illustrate, distinguishing complete sentences from fragments is not quite as straightforward as identifying the subject and the verb positioned between a capital letter and a full stop. The key is to read the sentence back to yourself and if it sounds as if there is something missing or something needs to be added then it is probably because it is not a complete sentence.

Rule 2

Recognizing the Subject and the Object in a Sentence

The Rule: Sentences, as we have seen, are usually constructed with a subject, a verb and an object. These sentences also have what is known as 'voices'. Namely an *active* voice or a *passive* voice.

The active voice is, in a sense, the natural voice we use to describe the world around us. This is the voice that we use most of the time when talking about things in the here and now. In the active voice, the **object** receives the action of the verb performed by the agent/subject:

Dogs bark at cats.

Dogs (subject) *bark* (verb) *at* (preposition) *cats* (object).

Active sentences are easy to spot as they follow the standard word order that we produce innately when making simple statements in the present. In the passive voice, the situation described remains essentially the same, except the

subject of the sentence swaps places with the object and becomes the recipient of the verb action.

Cats are barked at by dogs.

Cats (subject) *are barked* (verbs) *at by* (preposition) *dogs* (object).

There are two things to note when determining if a sentence is in the active voice or the passive voice. Firstly, if the sentence contains the word 'by' to determine who or what has performed the action then the sentence is passive:

Bleak House was written by Charles Dickens.

Secondly, if the sentence contains the auxiliary verb 'to be, and the past participle of the main verb (for a more detailed explanation of verb forms see *'How Much and How Many?'*). In the example above, 'was' is the past of 'to be' and 'written' the past participle of the main verb 'to write'. Sentences do not have to contain 'by' to be in the passive voice as one use of the passive voice is when the agent of the action described is either unknown or not stated:

I will be shot. (passive)

They will shoot me. (active)

Primary school teachers tend to discourage the use of the passive in written compositions. This is principally because certain sentences in the passive voice sound awkward and unwieldy ('I will be shot by them') and the active voice more dynamic and engaging to the reader. There are certain situations however, where using the passive voice has its uses and is perfectly permissible. As stated above, this is usually when the agent of the action is unknown or superfluous to the overall sense of the sentence. The passive voice can also be used to add emphasis to certain elements in a sentence that need to be foregrounded or highlighted. Warning signs are often written in passive form for this reason as in 'safety helmets must be worn at all times'. Conversely, the passive voice can also be used to de-emphasize who or what has done the action. This is particularly prevalent in the language of politics. The next time a news report contains phrases such as 'The minister told parliament that mistakes have been made', marvel at how skilfully blame has been subtly shifted away from the agent (the people or persons responsible for the mistakes) on to the mistakes themselves (as if that was at all possible).

In Summary

Try to use the active voice in writing as this will avoid ambiguity and make sentences more vibrant and appealing to the audience or reader. The passive should only be used if the agent of the action is unknown or superfluous to the intended meaning.

The Essential Tools
The Naming of Things

Nouns are naming words that describe people, places, objects or ideas. Within this broad lexis are sub-categories that describe more explicitly the type of naming word individual nouns represent.

Common Nouns: These are general/ non-specific names for objects, people, places and things e.g. *man, woman, book, mountain, city.*

Proper Nouns: These are more specifically defined names for people, places e.g. *New York, Mt Etna, Lady Gaga* and so on.

Concrete Nouns: These are phenomena that can be perceived via a combination of the human senses such as *rain, food, fruit, trees* etc.

Abstract Nouns: These are the opposite of concrete nouns in that they relate to concepts that cannot be directly perceived through the senses such as *love, belief, fear, destiny, pride* etc.

Nouns can also be divided into *countable* nouns (*one dog, two cats, ten million Quentins*) and things that are *uncountable* (*milk, water, music, snow, grass*), and nouns that are singular or plural (see Rule 3 and Rule 4).

Rule 3

❧

How to Use 'Much' and 'Many'

The Rule: When forming questions and statements relating to quantities and amounts of something, *many/fewer* is used with countable nouns and *much/less* with uncountable nouns.

❧

How much time do you spend thinking about grammar? How many times have you found yourself getting confused? Do you make fewer mistakes now you understand some of the essential rules? Is it much less of a problem now?

When we describe quantities and amounts of things, we commonly use words such as *many*, *much*, *less* and *fewer* in questions and positive and negative statements. Each of these quantifiers is attached, unsurprisingly, to a noun. The premise of which quantifier to use when, relates to whether the correlating noun is countable or uncountable. So, for example, most people don't waste *much time* worrying about grammar as they spend *many hours* worrying about other, possibly more important things. In this instance, time, as strange as it seems, is uncountable as it cannot be physically experienced. Units of time however, days, hours, minutes and seconds etc., can obviously be counted. The same is also true of nouns such as money, information and work:

I don't have much money, how many pounds can you lend me?

Too many jobs means too much work.

I have read many reports but don't have much information.

Nouns such as time, money, information and work are abstract nouns, things that exist as concepts and not tangible entities. It would be a mistake however, to assume that all abstract nouns are uncountable and so correlate with 'much' and 'less'. Some abstract nouns can be both countable and uncountable in the same way that some concrete nouns can be both countable and uncountable according to the context and meaning. For example:

*Does it take much **work** to read Hamlet, Shakespeare's greatest **work**?*

*We don't have many **rooms** in our apartment, so there isn't much **room** for visitors.*

In common speech, the phrase 'a lot of' is used with questions and statements and also takes both countable and uncountable nouns. For example:

A lot of people like to watch football. (countable)

I don't have a lot of time to watch football. (uncountable)

This basic rule also traditionally applies for the precise use of 'less' as the quantifier with uncountable nouns, singular amounts and volumes, and 'fewer' with countable, individual things and units. For example:

I should spend less money, otherwise I'll have fewer pounds left in the bank.

However, the rule has a grey area that causes confusion when applied in certain contexts. For example:

If I had drunk fewer beers last night, I wouldn't have a hangover.

The example above sounds rather cumbersome and awkward despite being grammatically correct and this is for two reasons. Firstly the noun 'beer' can be both countable and uncountable:

There are fewer beers being brewed these days than twenty years ago. (countable)

Less beer is sold in bars these days. (uncountable)

In the first sentence above, 'beers' refers to individual types of beer and so is a countable quantity. In the second sentence, beer is used in the general, uncountable sense, like water or milk or sugar. Returning to our friend here lamenting their overindulgence, it would sound more natural if they had said: 'If I had drunk less beer last night, I wouldn't have a hangover.' The reason for this grey area is that 'beer' in this context is taken to describe the sum total of units consumed within the specific time span ('last night'). 'Less' can therefore be used as a quantifier for numbers considered as stand alone, bulk amounts:

We are getting married in less than two weeks.

You can eat a three-course meal in Spain for less than ten euros.

In both of the examples above 'less' is quantifying a specified bulk amount as a single countable unit ('two weeks', 'ten euros') not describing the sum of their parts (individual weeks and euros). The Plain English Campaign (see page 38) has a basic formula to follow in that 'less' should be used to mean 'not as much' and 'fewer' should be used to mean 'not as many'. For example:

I drink less coffee these days.

I read fewer books these days.

How Many Items in the Basket?

In 2008, The Plain English Campaign, a charity devoted to 'campaigning against gobbledygook, jargon and misleading public information', lobbied the retail chain Tesco to change their checkout signs that stated '10 Items or Less'. Their argument followed the rule that 'less' should be used with uncountable nouns and that to be grammatically correct, the signs should state '10 Items or Fewer'. This caused some debate among linguists who adhere to the additional maxim that 'fewer' should also be used to mean 'not as many'. The confusion for shoppers obsessive about grammar was that '10 Items or Fewer' is contradictory and awkward and strictly speaking should read 'Fewer Than 10 Items' (a maximum of only nine items). In the end, Tesco settled for amending their signs to the more prosaic but seemingly clear-cut statement: 'Up To 10 Items'.

In Summary

'Much' should always correlate with uncountable nouns and 'many' with countable nouns; 'fewer' should be used to quantify numbers of separate items or people, 'less' is for quantities not thought of in numbers or for specified single bulk amounts.

Rule 4

⁂

The Spelling Conventions for Singular and Plural Nouns

The Rule: Regular nouns form their plural by adding 's' or 'es' to the singular. Irregular nouns form their plural by changing their endings in a variety of different ways or remaining the same in both singular and plural.

⁂

Forming plurals should be easy and for regular nouns it is, just add an 's' or an 'es' to the singular. Think 'fish/fishes'. But think again. Is 'fishes' really the plural of 'fish'? Do people not say by way of consolation to a friend whose relationship has ended 'There are plenty more fish in the sea'? As this statement is referring to the number of unattached single people looking for love, it should really be 'There are plenty more fishes in the sea'.

Fish is actually one of a small number of words that have two plurals, both a regular and an irregular form depending on the context. If we were writing a scientific paper on marine biology and wanted to describe the variety of species of fish found in Australia's Great Barrier Reef we may use the plural 'fishes'. If we wanted to describe the number of stingrays that are found in the aforementioned reef collectively we may use the plural 'fish'.

Irregular nouns form their plural in the following ways:

Words that end in the letter 'f', substitute the last letter with 've' before adding an 's':

> elf (singular)/elves (plural)
> wolf/wolves
> loaf/loaves

Words that end in 'y' where the previous letter is a consonant substitute the 'y' for an 'i' before adding the suffix 'es' as in 'lady/ladies'.

Some nouns form their irregular plural by adding the letters 'en' or 'ren' as in 'ox/oxen' or 'child/children'.

Some nouns form their irregular plural by altering their principal vowel sound:

> foot/feet
> man/men
> woman/women
> goose/geese

There are also certain nouns, mostly animal names that retain their singular form as the plural: sheep, deer, cod and mackerel. There are also certain nouns that can only be used in the plural and this is because either they are things comprised of two integral parts, as in scissors or trousers or glasses (we often refer to these in 'pairs' as in 'a pair of pyjamas') or we are referring to something as a totality in itself such as ashes or remains. N.M. Gwynne, in his book, *Gwynne's Grammar*, also adds 'embers' to this latter category but this is to deny the evocative line in Edgar Allan Poe's poem *The Raven*:

'Ah, distinctly I remember it was in the bleak December,
And each separate dying <u>ember</u> wrought its ghost upon
the floor.'

One of the principal confusions with plurals springs from words that have been absorbed into English from other languages. Over time, these words from classical languages such as Greek and Latin, have become anglicized and their plural forms have altered accordingly. Words such as formula, focus or forum can take an informal plural such as formulas, focuses or forums, although originally their plurals were irregular: formulae, foci and fora. Academic and in particular, scientific writing, tends to favour the older plural forms of such nouns, probably because they add a certain gravitas and quality of expression. In everyday speech however, to talk of 'the foci of my studies in English grammar' would sound somewhat pretentious and the *Oxford English Dictionary* states that both plural forms are acceptable in either formal or informal circumstances. This process of anglicizing or standardizing words that have entered into English from other languages also works in reverse in that there are also some irregular nouns where the original plural form is now taken as the singular such as confetti or graffiti and data, which has completely lost its original singular form 'datum'.

Luca Brasi Sleeps With The Fish?

In one of the most famous scenes from Francis Ford Coppola's film *The Godfather*, Sonny Corleone (played by James Caan) receives a message from a rival mobster in the form of a dead fish wrapped in paper. The fish is a sign that the rival gang has murdered the Corleone family's principal hit man. 'It's a Sicilian message, it means Luca Brasi sleeps with the fishes' explains one of the gangsters. This is, of course, incorrect, and the message should have been 'Luca Brasi sleeps with the fish' in the collective sense, unless of course 'the fishes' is a euphemism for the number of mafia victims whose bodies have been dumped in the Hudson River. It is probably not advisable to correct violent gangsters on their grammar however, unless you want to wake up with a horse's head next to you.

In Summary

Any confusion about the correct irregular plural form to use in formal writing can be easily cleared up by recourse to any decent dictionary. Be mindful of overcomplicating writing by reaching for what you consider to be the correct form when a simpler form is probably sufficient. The danger is that, for example, you may wish to be speaking about spending time searching the indices of books in the library when really you meant to be searching through the indexes.

The Essential Tools
Being and Doing:
The Business of Verbs

Verbs are the most complex of all the parts of speech and in many ways the most important. Put bluntly, sentences cannot function without verbs. For example 'Jesus Saves' displayed on a poster outside a church is a sentence; take away the verb 'saves' and 'Jesus' on his own, is not, strictly speaking, a sentence.

A verb is a word that describes an action or state of being and in terms of sentence constructions can be divided into two types: transitive verbs and intransitive verbs. However, most verb forms can be either transitive or intransitive, depending on the structure of the sentence they appear in. Transitive verbs appear in sentences that contain a subject noun and an object noun, for example:

Dave (subject noun) *looked* (transitive verb) *at the sea* (object noun).

An intransitive verb is a verb in a sentence that either does not require an object or omits an object, for example:

Dave (subject) *looked* (intransitive verb).

Here are some more examples so you can see the difference between transitive and intransitive verbs:

Beckham (subject noun) *kicked* (transitive verb) *the ball straight at the wall* (object noun).

He lived (intransitive verb), *he loved* (intransitive verb*), he died* (intransitive verb).

She screamed (intransitive verb).

I (subject noun) *went* (transitive verb) *swimming yesterday* (adverb/object noun).

We (subject noun) *ate* (transitive verb) *our lunch* (object noun) *in a lovely restaurant.*

Rule 5

How to Spot the Difference Between Regular and Irregular Verbs

<u>The Rule:</u> The past forms of irregular verbs either change completely from the base form (the infinitive) or remain the same in all three forms, or the past forms change from the infinitive but the simple and participle forms do not end in 'ed'.

Verbs come in a variety of different classes: *regular* and *irregular*, *principal* and *auxiliary*. And all verbs have three basic forms: *infinitive*, *simple past* and *past participle*. Regular verbs are verbs where the past forms (simple and participle) are made by adding 'ed' or 'd' if the verb ends in an 'e'.

Examples of Regular Verbs

Infinitive / Base Form	Past Simple	Past Participle
To work	worked	worked
To study	studied*	studied*
To believe	believed	believed
To change	changed	changed
To discuss	discussed	discussed
To debate	debated	debated
To enjoy*	enjoyed	enjoyed

* Verbs that end in 'y' in the base form replace the 'y' with 'ied' in the past forms, with the exception of 'enjoyed'.

Irregular verbs are therefore verbs that do not end in 'ed' or verbs where the infinitive/base form doesn't change in the past forms (such as 'to hit', 'to put' or 'to saw'.)

Examples of Irregular Verbs

Infinitive/ Base Form	Past Simple	Past Participle
To begin	began	begun
To wake	woke	woken
To eat	ate	eaten
To come	came	come
To drink	drank	drunk
To cut	cut	cut
To read	read	read

This all seems very simple and straightforward – ends in 'ed' or 'd' in past form = regular, everything else = irregular. But as ever with English there are exceptions and pitfalls:

1. Some verbs can be both regular and irregular, for example:

    learn, **learned**, learned
    learn, **learnt**, learnt

2. Some verbs change their meaning depending on whether they are regular or irregular, for example 'to hang':

regular	hang, hanged, hanged	To kill or die, by dropping with a rope around the neck.
irregular	hang, hung, hung	To fix something (for example, a picture) at the top so that the lower part is free.

3. The present tense (see Rule 6) of some regular verbs is the same as the past tense of some irregular verbs:

regular	found, founded, founded	To create an organization or institution.
irregular	find, found, found	To discover something or someone that has been lost, hidden or undiscovered.

In addition to regular and irregular verbs, verbs can also be classed as **principal verbs** and **auxiliary verbs** that combine to produce **compound verb forms**. Principal verbs are the main active verb and auxiliary verbs modify the main verb, often to form tenses to determine when the action or state happened, happens or will happen or to predict, speculate or hypothesize about an action. For example:

I have been working hard lately.

The tense *have been working* is formed by the auxiliary verbs **have** and **been** and the principal verb **working** because the present participle of 'to work' is the main action of the sentence.

In Summary

There aren't really any hard and fast rules for irregular verb forms so they just have to be learned by heart. Thankfully this isn't much of a problem for native English speakers who produce the correct forms innately (although the odd gaff creeps in with past participles: 'swum' being an example as 'have swam' sounds like it should be correct but it isn't). There are also American-English variations that sound awkward to the British ear but are commonplace in the US and Canada, most notably, the past participle of 'got': 'I have *gotten* a new job.'

Rule 6

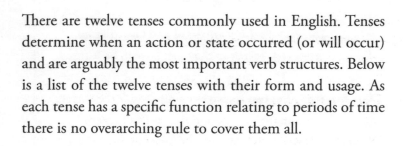

Don't Feel Tense About the Tenses

<u>The Rule:</u> The term 'tense', in traditional approaches to grammar, relates to the conjugation (the different forms) of a verb used to indicate the time frame: past, present, or future, of the continuance or completion of an action or state.

There are twelve tenses commonly used in English. Tenses determine when an action or state occurred (or will occur) and are arguably the most important verb structures. Below is a list of the twelve tenses with their form and usage. As each tense has a specific function relating to periods of time there is no overarching rule to cover them all.

Present Simple

The present simple tense for the most part (see the exception below) remains the same as the base form of the verb (the infinitive) and is used to determine the here and now, regular repeated actions and things that are always true. For example:

I swim.

I swim on Sundays.

Fish swim in the sea.

The principal exception is the verb 'to be', which takes the following irregular forms:

I am / you are / he or she is / they are / was / were

Present Continuous

When we describe actions in the present we rarely mean a specific point in time, but an ongoing or series of actions occurring at the time of speaking and this is expressed with the present continuous tense:

*I **am reading** the newspaper.*

The present continuous sentence here (sometimes called *present progressive*) is formed with the auxiliary verb 'to be' and the present participle or *ing* form of the verb. The present continuous is used informally in speech to describe soon to be occurring actions or future plans as in 'I am playing football on Sunday'.

Present Perfect

One of the most complicated tenses to teach to non-native speakers, the present perfect has several different functions and uses in different contexts. On a base level, the present perfect relates to the *unfinished* time of an action either leading up to the present or recently completed prior to the present *point of speaking*. The emphasis on *point of speaking* is key as one of the uses of the present perfect is to talk about completed actions in the past that have some import or impact upon the present. Imagine the scenario of a job interview for work in a restaurant. The interviewer asks the applicant the question 'What experience do you have?' and the applicant replies, 'I have worked in several restaurants as a sous chef'. Is the applicant working as a sous chef now at the *point of speaking* – obviously not. Is the applicant still working as a sous chef at another restaurant? Possibly, possibly not. However, the present perfect is used because the past experience or action has direct relevance to the present at the point of speaking.

Another usage of the present perfect is to describe an action in the past that is not time specific. For example:

> *'Have you ever been to Paris?'*
> *'Yes I have been to Paris.'*

The suggestion here is that time is *unfinished* because the person speaking is still alive and the action in the past is unspecified.

The present perfect is formed with the present auxiliary verb 'to have' (or *has*) and the past participle of the principal verb (in this case the verb 'to be' – *been*):

> *I **have been** to Paris.*

Present Perfect Continuous

As if the present perfect wasn't confusing enough, the second perfect tense in present form is the present perfect continuous and this is used to express a continuous action from the recent past that has just been completed prior to the point of speaking, or has continued up to this point and may continue into the future. For example:

> *I **have been teaching** for twenty years.*

The present perfect continuous is formed with *have/has* + the past participle of the verb 'to be' (*been*) and the present participle (ing) of the principal verb (in this case *teaching*).

Past Simple

The past simple tense is used to describe an action that has occurred in the past and has finished or a repeated completed action in the past. For example:

*I **played** cricket every day for a month.*

*I **lived** in Paris for five years.*

The past simple is formed with the past tense and is formed by adding 'ed' or 'd' with regular verbs but takes on different forms with irregular verbs (see Irregular Verbs on page 47).

Past Continuous

The past continuous tense is used to describe an action in the past that took a period of time to complete or an action that was ongoing at a fixed point in the past. For example:

Miss Marple: 'What were you doing on the night Professor Plum was murdered?'

*Miss Scarlet: 'I **was having** dinner with Reverend Green.'*

The past continuous is formed with the past tense of the auxiliary verb 'to be' and the present participle of the principal verb. In the example above, the verb 'to have' is the principal verb and not an auxiliary in this instance.

Past Perfect

Sometimes referred to as the *pluperfect* tense by fusty grammarians with a taste for Latin (pluperfect meaning 'beyond perfect'), the past perfect tense describes a past event that took place prior to another event or point in the past and is one of the principal tenses used in constructing narratives and ordering past events. For example:

*I **had started** the lesson when the fire alarm went off.*

The past perfect is formed by the past tense auxiliary verb 'had' and the past participle of the principal verb (in this case the regular verb 'to start').

Past Perfect Continuous

The past perfect continuous performs similar functions as the past continuous in that it expresses actions in the past taking place over a period of time but is also commonly used to express a continuous action leading up to another past event. For example:

> I **had been teaching** for twenty minutes when the fire alarm went off.

The past perfect continuous has a similar structure as the present perfect continuous but substitutes the past tense of the auxiliary verbs 'to have' (*had*) and 'to be' (*been*) before adding the present participle 'ing' form of the principal verb (in this case *teaching*).

Future Simple

Future tenses are used to describe or predict something that will, may or might occur at a point in time henceforth. Future tenses use specific verb forms known as 'modal auxiliary verbs' and these determine the extent to which something may or may not occur. Verbs such as *can, could, may, might, shall, should, will,* and *would* are all classified as modal auxiliary verbs but *will* and *shall* are used to form future tenses with other modals describing a variety of different structures and functions from making predictions to hypothesizing. The simple future is used to make predictions of future events or to express future plans and is formed with the auxiliary verb *will* or *shall* and the base form of the principal verb. For example:

*Cinderella, you **shall go** to the ball.*

Future Continuous

The future continuous tense is used to express an action that will be continuing for a period of time in the future. It is formed with *will* or *shall* and (in keeping with other continuous tenses) the auxilliary verb 'to be' with the present participle 'ing' form. For example:

*I **will be teaching** in Thailand this time next year.*

Future Perfect

The future perfect tense is used to predict or estimate future actions to be completed at some pre-determined point in the future and in common with all perfect tenses it is formed with the auxiliary verb 'to have' and the past participle of the principal verb following *will/shall*. For example:

*I **will have read** this book by Friday.*

Future Perfect Continuous

Probably the most obscure of the twelve tenses and hence, used in a rather specialized abstraction, the future perfect continuous relates to ongoing actions in the future over a period of time, often leading up to another action or point in the future. For example:

I **will have been waiting** for five hours.

I **will have been waiting** for five hours by the time you arrive.

The form for the future perfect continuous is the same as for the present perfect continuous but prefixed by will/shall.

Rule 7

❦

Dangling Participles Mangle Meaning

The Rule: A dangling participle is a modifying word that is in the wrong place in a sentence for the noun it is intended to describe, leading to ambiguous or scrambled meaning.

❦

A participle is a verb form that can act like an adjective, such as 'reading' or 'writing'. A participial phrase is used to describe an action, such as 'reading in the library' or 'writing on the wall' and modifies a noun in clauses or sentences.

One of the functions of participles (present and past) is to establish dependent (subordinate) clauses, which as we have seen in Rule 1, add additional information to modify the main clause. Problems occur when the modifier is either placed too far away from the person or thing it is meant to be describing, or other nouns or pronouns have sneaked into its place. In grammatical terms this is known as 'a dangling participle'.

Read the following sentences and consider who or what is doing the action described:

1. *After festering in the fridge for three days, my mother took out the cabbage and cooked it for supper.*

2. *While travelling to London, the weather deteriorated.*

3. *Flying high above, I had a great view of the kestrel hunting its prey.*

Sentence 1 suggests, somewhat unkindly, that my mother has been festering in the fridge for three days before deciding to cook cabbage for supper. In sentence 2, the weather appears to be travelling to London. In sentence 3, it appears I have mastered the ability to fly like Superman. The reason for the ambiguity and confusion in the examples above is that we naturally expect modifying participles to be placed in obvious proximity to the person, place or thing they are describing. If they are left dangling then the reader is also left dangling, or at the very least left scratching their heads.

One method to determine if a participle is dangling is to rejig the sentence by placing the participle directly after the subject of the sentence. For example:

The weather deteriorated while travelling to London.

If the new sentence sounds awkward and illogical then it is because the old sentence had a dangler that had crept in unnoticed.

A) *Driving round the corner, the Golden Gate Bridge reared suddenly into view.*

B) *The Golden Gate Bridge reared suddenly into view driving round the corner.*

Although both sentences have scrambled meaning, the rejig test in sentence B makes the nonsense all the more apparent. The problem is that the subject pronoun is missing from the main clause in the sentence. Who was driving round the corner? Thus, deprived of this vital piece of information, the suggestion is that it was San Francisco's most famous landmark at the wheel of a vehicle. The addition of a subject pronoun such as 'he', 'she' or 'I' to the sentence helps clarify any odd ambiguity:

As she was driving round the corner, the Golden Gate Bridge reared suddenly into view.

The trick is to ensure that the action in the sentence is actually connected to the person or thing doing it. It is an easy mistake to make when striving for conciseness and rhythm in written language. Lets look at an earlier scenario again and see how it could develop and be cured:

Having eaten the festering cabbage, my mother was surprised that I was taken ill.

This throws up a further ambiguity for if this sentence was spoken to somebody informally the meaning would probably be quite clear and deduced from context. In its current written form the participial phrase 'having eaten' is still left dangling so it appears that it was my mother who ate the cabbage. There are several ways to rewrite the sentence but the easiest way is to insert the missing pronoun that the participle is supposed to be modifying and replace 'having eaten' with an appropriate tense (in this case the past perfect):

*After **I had eaten** the festering cabbage, my mother was surprised that I was taken ill.*

Dangling participles appear in print with alarming regularity and this is largely due to journalists, writing to tight deadlines, attempting to cram as much information as they can into as few possible words. While there is obviously a place for concise, fine writing, trying to cut corners by starting sentences with participial phrases such as 'having been' can cause confusion.

In Summary

In order to avoid dangling participles ensure that the modifier is either preceded or followed by the noun(s) or pronoun(s) they are intended to modify. If still unsure, rewrite the sentence substituting the participial phrase for a suitable tense and noun/pronoun.

For example:

Having set out the picnic, the rain started immediately.
The rain started immediately after we (had) set out the picnic.

The Essential Tools
Adverbs – It Ain't What You Do It's The Way That You Do It!

Adverbs are divided into four categories, each determined by a specific function within a sentence:

Adverbs of Manner

Adverbs of manner communicate *how* **something happened.** They are generally used to modify verbs. In the sentence, they appear after the verb or after the object. They should not be placed between the verb and its object:

*The boy laughed **loudly**.*

*Elena did a pirouette **gracefully**.*

Not: *Elena did **gracefully** a pirouette.*

An adverb of manner can be placed at the beginning of a sentence or before a verb and object to make the statement stronger. For example:

Gracefully, Elena did a pirouette.

*Elena **gracefully** did a pirouette.*

Adverbs of manner are used with active verbs, those that show action. They are not used with stative verbs, verbs that show a state of being. For example:

Not: *Elena seemed **gracefully**.*

'Seem' is a stative verb and does not show action. It does not, therefore, take an adverb of manner. To determine whether an adverb is one of manner, ask a 'how' question: How did the boy laugh? How did Elena do a pirouette?

Adverbs of Time

Adverbs of time tell us *when* **something happened.** They can also tell us for how long or how frequently something happened. They are generally used to modify verbs. 'When' adverbs usually come at the end of a sentence. One exception is 'still', which appears before the main verb in a sentence. For example:

*Let's meet **then**.*

*The package arrived **yesterday**.*

*Mike and Dave have swimming lessons **weekly**.*

*They are **still** learning the basics.*

To determine if an adverb is one of time, ask a 'when' question or a 'how long/how often' question. For example:

When shall we meet?

When did the package arrive?

How often do Mike and Dave have swimming lessons?

A word of warning about using 'yet'. This adverb of time is only used in questions and negative statements. For example:

*'Have you finished your homework **yet**?'*

*'I have not finished it **yet**.'*

Not: *'I have finished it **yet**.'*

Adverbs of Degree

Adverbs of degree tell us the *extent or intensity* **to which something happened.** They can modify verbs, adjectives or other adverbs. Adverbs of degree are generally placed before the main verb or the adjective or adverb they modify. For example:

*She was **entirely** wrong in her judgement.*

*He drove **very** quickly.*

*Clarisse **thoroughly** believes he is innocent.*

*She is **too** stubborn to change her mind.*

To determine if an adverb is one of degree, ask a to 'what degree' or 'how much' question. For example:

To what degree was she wrong in her judgement?

To what degree did he drive?

How much does Clarisse believe he is innocent?

One exception to adverb placement is 'enough', which appears after an adjective or adverb that it modifies. For example:

*Are you warm **enough**?*

*Am I working quickly **enough**?*

Adverbs of Place

Adverbs of place tell us *where* **something happened.** They are generally used to modify verbs and appear after the main verb or after the object in a sentence. For example:

*I'll meet you **there** after class.*

*She would go **anywhere** with him.*

*Victor put the book **away**.*

To determine if an adverb is one of place, ask a 'where' question. For example:

Where will I meet you after class?

Where would she go with him?

Where did Victor put the book?

Rule 8

'Neither/Nor' and 'Either/Or' Must Always be Used Together

<u>The Rule:</u> **When describing a choice between two possibilities 'either' is paired with 'or' in positive sentences and 'neither' with 'nor' in negative sentences. If both subject nouns are singular then the corresponding verb must be singular, if one (or both) of the elements is plural then the corresponding verb must also be plural.**

It appears from the outset that the rule pairing the use of 'neither' and 'nor' and 'either' and 'or' is straightforward. It is however, a common mistake in everyday speech, partly because 'nor' seems slightly archaic and cumbersome. 'Neither my father *or* my mother went to college' sounds natural enough despite being incorrect.

The element of the rule that causes the most confusion is ensuring that the subject of the structure agrees with its verb. For example:

*Either my mother or my father **is** going to give me a lift home.*

As 'mother' and 'father' are singular subject nouns the verb 'is' must be 'in agreement', as grammarians like to say, and be a singular verb.

Similarly, if one or both of the subject nouns is plural then the following verb must 'agree' and also be plural:

*Neither my father nor my **brothers are** going to give me a lift home.*

An 'either . . . or' or 'neither . . . nor' construction can include more than two elements, but some grammar guides advise writers to restrict the usage to reference to two choices: 'I'm going to wear either blue or green' but not 'I'm going to wear either blue, green, or red.' If you agree with that restriction delete '*either*' from the latter sentence — and it's optional in the first one, for that matter. Omitting '*neither*' is not an option in the sentence 'I'm going to wear neither blue nor green' but the idea can also be rendered 'I'm not going to wear blue or green.' The proscription against using '*or*', rather than '*nor*', with '*neither*' ('I was neither here or there' instead of 'I was neither here nor there') is likewise not absolute, but '*nor*' is most common.

The third divergence is about agreement with a verb. The more restrictive rule is that when '*either*' or '*neither*' is the subject, or part of the subject, of a sentence or a clause, it should be accompanied by a singular verb: 'I don't think either of the candidates is qualified. When two nouns or pronouns are framed by *'either'* and *'or'*, use a singular verb if the noun or pronoun closest to the verb is singular ('Either the boys or the girl is responsible') and a plural verb if the closest noun or pronoun is plural ('Either the girl or the boys are responsible') or both nouns or pronouns are plural ('Either the girls or the boys are responsible').

However, it is common to see a plural verb with *'either'* or *'neither'* in reference to a sole plural noun or pronoun, as in 'Neither of the parties are willing to compromise.' The more conservative choice is to write 'Neither of the parties is willing to compromise.' Here are several other considerations: when constructing an 'either ... or' or a 'neither ... nor' statement, take care to place verbs appropriately. If one verb applies to both choices, place it before the 'either ... or' phrase: 'She was going to leave either tomorrow or Saturday.' If a separate verb applies to each choice, *'either'* should precede the first verb, and *'or'* should come before the second one: 'She was going to either leave tomorrow or wait until Saturday.' Also, avoid using a 'not ... either' phrase, as in 'They will not vote on either the amended proposal or the original one.'; revise it to a 'neither ... nor' construction: 'They will vote on neither the amended proposal nor the original one.'

Finally, a statement that two things are not true can also be rendered with a 'never ... nor' construction: 'Their facility had never completed an evaluation nor ever met anyone representing the contracting agency.'

In Summary

This is really a matter of maintaining consistency in sentences or, in linguistic jargon, keeping sentences parallel. A parallel sentence is one that is balanced and one in which the elements conform with each other. Hence, 'neither' should be matched with 'nor' and 'either' with 'or', and the two forms should not be interchanged.

Rule 9

❈

Try Not to Ever Split Infinitives

The Rule: The infinitive form of a verb is preceded by the particle 'to': *to run, to jump*. To split an infinitive is to put an adverb between the 'to' and the 'verb' when it should go either immediately before or after them.

❈

There are few grammar bugbears more likely *to broadly split* opinion than spliced infinitives. On one hand, champions of correct English object to the splitting of infinitives with an adverb or adverbial phrase on the grounds that it betrays an inelegance of style. However, the opposing camp argue precisely the opposite, claiming that overzealous adherence to avoiding split infinitives at all costs can lead at times to awkward or ambiguous sentence structures. Probably the most famous split infinitive in popular culture is the voice-over at the beginning of the *Star Trek* television series:

*Space: the final frontier. These are the voyages of The Starship Enterprise. Its five-year mission: to explore strange new worlds, to seek out new life and new civilizations, **to boldly go** where no man has gone before.*

73

It is debatable that this iconic phrase would have quite the same resonance if rewritten as 'boldly to go' or 'to go boldly'. Interestingly, the producers of the *Star Trek* franchise corrected the split infinitive for the title sequence of 1991 film *Star Trek VI: The Undiscovered Country* to 'boldly going . . .' and received hundreds of irate letters from disgruntled Trekkies. Subsequent films in the series have reverted back to the original.

Here are some more examples of split infinitives:

'To strongly, wrongly, vainly love thee still.'

'Love And Death', Lord Byron

'What ever have been thought on in this state,
That could be brought to bodily act ere Rome
Had circumvention?'

Coriolanus, Act I, Scene II
William Shakespeare

The main point of contention is that the splitting of infinitives is common practice in everyday speech. Politicians appear on television stating that they expect 'the economy *to steadily grow*' or for 'the number of people unemployed *to dramatically fall*' and few people either notice or actually care. If the latter statement is rewritten as 'the number of people unemployed *to fall dramatically*' it would still mean the same thing.

However, there are times when splitting infinitives produces an ambiguous sentence or unintentional comic effect and conversely, not splitting the infinitive changes the emphasis of the sentence:

1. *I told him to seriously consider my offer.*

2. *I told him to consider my offer seriously.*

In the first sentence, I am suggesting that the person in question gives considerable thought to my offer. The second sentence, suggests that the person in question may think I am joking.

> *'Would you convey my compliments to the purist*
> *who reads your proofs and tell him or her that*
> *. . . when I split an infinitive, God damn it,*
> *I split it so it will stay split.'*

Raymond Chandler

The History Behind The Rule

The rule that 'to' should not be separated from the verb in a sentence is often thought of as a hangover from scholars of classical languages such as Greek and Latin in which it is impossible to divide an infinitive verb. However, this argument relies on the supposition that there are direct parallels between Latin grammar and English grammar. Although the majority of English words are derived from Latin, English grammar is not, therefore it is nonsensical to apply Latin grammar to English structures.

It is interesting then to note that the first recorded objections to split infinitives began to appear in grammar texts in the mid-nineteenth century. The Victorian era saw a huge explosion in the publication and popularity of grammar books. Debates about correct English usage can be seen as a reaction to the development of the state education system and landmark acts of parliament such as The Elementary Education Act of 1870 that made attending school compulsory for the first time. The question of what was 'right' and what was 'not right' in the teaching of grammar spawned many heated arguments amongst academics and amateur pedants alike.

> *'Your fatuous specialist is now beginning to rebuke 'second-rate' newspapers for using such phrases as 'to suddenly go' and 'to boldly say'. I ask you, Sir, to put this man out without interfering with his perfect freedom of choice between 'to suddenly go', 'to go suddenly' and 'suddenly to go'. Set him adrift and try an intelligent Newfoundland dog in his place.'*

George Bernard Shaw

In Summary

As a general rule it is probably best to avoid splitting infinitives in formal writing, but it is perfectly acceptable in more informal usage or when writing to entertain. Adverbs add colour and rhythm to prose, and the flow of a sentence can be disrupted or jar if we slavishly refuse *to never split* an infinitive. Use your judgement and go with whatever gives the best reading.

The Essential Tools
Problems with Pronouns

Pronouns have a variety of different functions but at a base level they replace and/or moderate nouns. For example:

> *David Beckham has been voted Britain's best dressed man because **he** takes great pride in his appearance.*

The eight subcategories of pronouns are as follows:

Personal Pronouns that replace common and proper nouns such as: *I, me, you, him, her, them, they* etc. These can be used as the subject or object of a sentence.

Relative Pronouns that link subordinate clauses in sentences such as: *that, which, who, whom* etc.

Demonstrative Pronouns that relate to a specific thing or things such as *this* book, *that* meal etc. Demonstrative pronouns also perform the same function as demonstrative adjectives and so are both pronoun and adjective simultaneously.

Indefinite Pronouns that refer to unspecified people or objects such as: *anybody, anything, nobody, some, many, several* etc.

Reflexive Pronouns that we use when speaking about *ourselves* or *yourself.*

Interrogative Pronouns that are used to ask questions and gather information such as: *who, whose, which, what* and *whom?*

Reciprocal Pronouns that are used to describe relationships between two people or things such as: *one another* and *each other.*

Possessive Pronouns that denote ownership in the first, second and third person such as: *mine, yours, his, hers, ours* and *theirs.* Possessive pronouns also perform the same function as possessive adjectives in that they describe who the noun belongs to.

Rule 10

───❦───

The Correct Use of 'That' and 'Which'

The Rule: In defining relative clauses 'that' is considered to be correct and commas are not required to separate the composite parts of the sentence. In non-defining relative clauses, 'which' is preceded by a comma to separate the composite parts of the sentence.

───❦───

One of the bewildering aspects of technical grammar (and there are many) is a tendency for grammarians to adopt different terminology to describe the same thing. On more than one occasion I have been asked by a perplexed student to explain the difference between the present perfect continuous and the present perfect progressive. The answer is that there isn't any difference, the same tense, just different names. The same problem occurs when approaching relative clauses. Are they 'defining relative clauses' or are they 'restrictive relative clauses'? For the purposes of consistency with the rule concerning the use of 'that' and 'which' as relative pronouns, I have chosen the term 'defining'. The term 'restrictive' is more common in traditional grammar circles but I don't feel it is particularly helpful in explaining a complex subject.

The Same Sentence, Different Meanings

The tricky aspect to grasp with regard to defining and non-defining clauses is how the merest insertion of a comma can subtly change the meaning of a sentence.

Consider the following sentences:

My son who went to Cambridge University has a good job.

My son, who went to Cambridge University, has a good job.

How many sons do I have? In sentence one, I have more than one son as the absence of commas creates a 'defining' relative clause. I am making a clear distinction between my son who went to Cambridge and my son(s) who didn't. In sentence two, the insertion of the commas creates a 'non-defining' relative clause. I have only one son and I am rightfully proud of his achievements so have decided to add some additional information and show off about it. The trick is to decide if the sentence can be split into two independent statements. The second sentence could feasibly be rewritten as: *My son went to Cambridge University. He has a good job.* The first sentence can't without losing some of its intended meaning. Therefore, the second sentence is non-defining as the commas separate additional information.

'Which' Versus 'That'

These subtle nuances of meaning are further complicated by the choice of relative pronoun in the clause. 'Who' or 'whom' is required for people (see Rule 10), 'which' or 'that' for things, and 'that' for people in defining relative clauses (although this is frowned upon in some circles).

Consider the following sentences and the difference in meaning:

My kittens that are black are frightened to go outside.

My kittens, which are black, are frightened to go outside.

How many kittens do I have and what colour are they? It is impossible to know how many kittens I have in either sentence, other than more than one. With regard to colour, the suggestion is that in sentence one, I have other kittens, possibly ginger or tabby, who aren't frightened to go outside. In sentence two, all of my kittens are black and all of them are frightened to go outside (note how sentence two can be split into two stand-alone statements). The rule governing the use of 'which' or 'that', according to various newspaper style guides, is to use 'which' in a generalized sense to *add* additional information and to use 'that' in a specific, *defining* sense. Hence, 'that' should be applied to defining relative clauses (omitting commas) and 'which' to non-defining relative clauses as in the example of my kittens. It isn't really important what colour the kittens are, I just thought you might like to know that they are black.

Problems occur when the two relative pronouns are misplaced or confused. This often occurs in common speech without too many catastrophic misunderstandings, as the correct meaning is usually inferred through context and intonation. In written English however, such slippages can cause ambiguities. For example:

Computer games, which are violent, shouldn't be sold to under-eighteens.

Although grammatically correct in terms of being a non-defining relative clause, not all computer games are violent and surely it was the intention to define violent games as the ones to be restricted? One way to safety check the use of 'which' or 'that' is to decide if the clause in question can be left out altogether without losing the general meaning. To return to the kittens again: 'My kittens are frightened to go outside' (*which* has nothing to do with their colour). The issues surrounding computer games in the sentence above however, require the clause to make sense of the statement. 'Computer games shouldn't be sold to under-eighteens' is a different proposition.

The reality that he couldn't sing, which was obvious to anyone who heard him, didn't deter him from trying.

In the example above, our tone-deaf singer is either oblivious to his vocal shortcomings or just doesn't care what other people think. Thus, the clause can be omitted without radically altering the sense of the sentence: 'The reality that he couldn't sing didn't deter him from trying,' and rightfully so too!

In Summary

Always use 'that' when referring to a person or a thing in specific circumstances. Use 'which' preceded by a comma with clauses providing additional information that is non-essential to the overall sense of the sentence.

Rule 11

---❧---

When to Use 'Who' and 'Whom'

The Rule: 'Who' should be used as the subject
of the verb in a sentence and 'whom' as the
object and following a preposition.

---❧---

'Who' and 'whom' are relative and interrogative pronouns that cause all sorts of problems in formal written English. Correcting errors with who and whom is a pastime much beloved by grammar pedants and although the rules governing correct usage are fairly clear-cut, even experienced writers lack confidence, particularly when using 'whom'. The reason for this is that 'whom' is rarely used in informal speech, with 'who' seeming to be much more natural. Consider the scenario of answering the telephone in a busy office. Most people are much more likely to ask the person on the end of the line the question 'Who do you wish to speak to?' Rather than the somewhat stiff and stuffy 'To whom do you wish to speak?'

In deciding which word to use it is first necessary to identify the subject and the object in the sentences or clauses. The subject, remember, is who or what is doing the action described by the verb, and the object is who or what the action is being done to, or is directly affected by the verb. It should be noted that not all principal verbs have direct objects in sentences. In the sentence, 'Who made the cake?' 'Who' is the subject of the sentence. In the sentence 'The cake was made by whom?' the relative pronoun 'whom' has become the object of the sentence and takes the preposition 'by' (for more on prepositions see pages 135–136 and Rule 18).

This is straightforward in simple sentences but becomes considerably more tricky when dealing with complex sentences with multiple clauses. The trick in this case is to break the separate clauses down into separate sentences. For example:

The boys, three of whom were under age, were taken into police custody.

The boys were taken into police custody.
Three of them were under age.

Notice that in breaking the clauses down into separate sentences I have slightly rewritten it by substituting 'them' for 'whom' and this is a test that can be used to determine which form is correct to use. First remove 'who' or 'whom' from the clause and replace with the correct pronoun, either subject pronoun (*I, you, he, she, it, we,* or *they*) or object pronoun (*me, you, him, her, it, us* or *them*). Let's give it a try:

*Kylie Minogue, **whom** you met in the nightclub, is a celebrity.*

Kylie Minogue is a celebrity.
You met her in the nightclub.

So you would use 'whom' as you met 'her', you didn't meet 'she'.

Many people would quite naturally say 'who you met in a nightclub' and hardly anyone would notice the error. The confusion is that Kylie Minogue is the subject of the overall sentence but she is also the object of the verb 'met' so whom is correct. If we apply our pronoun test, 'you met she in the nightclub' is clearly incorrect and as her is an object pronoun, 'whom' must be the correct form.

The man, who hasn't been named, died on the way to the hospital.

The man died on the way to hospital.
He hasn't been named.

So it is correct to use 'who' as 'he' hasn't been named, not 'his'. Here again, 'he' is a subject pronoun so 'who' must be correct. The same test can also be used when 'who' or 'whom' are used in question forms:

Who broke the vase?
He did!

Or,

The vase was broken by whom?
It was broken by him!

A Whom's Who of Literature

There are numerous examples of great writers confusing 'who' and 'whom' in relative clauses and sentences, ranging from John Donne to Graham Greene. In 1923, *The Oxford English Dictionary* cited an example from Thomas Hardy's *Far From The Madding Crowd* as being in error for using the phrase 'Who are you speaking of?', only to later decide that as it was a rendering of colloquial speech is was in fact probably correct. P.G. Wodehouse gently pokes fun at the 'who' versus 'whom' issue in his novel *Thank You, Jeeves* (1934):

> *"'Oh, I'm not complaining," said Chuffy, looking rather like Saint Sebastian on receipt of about the fifteenth arrow. "You have a perfect right to love who you like . . ."*
> *"Whom, old man," I couldn't help saying. Jeeves has made me rather a purist in these matters.'*

The joke is that, strictly speaking, Bertie Wooster is wrong and the proper correction should be 'You have the perfect right to love *whomever* you like'.

In an entry into his diary, Russian writer Anton Chekhov manages to skilfully use both forms in the same sentence:

> *'How unbearable at times are people **who** are happy,*
> *people for **whom** everything works out.'*

How unbearable at times are people who are clever, people for whom the complexities of language seem easy!

In Summary

Decide which pronoun to replace 'who' or 'whom' with in the sentence or the clause and if a subject pronoun works (*I, you, he, she, it, we,* or *they*) then use 'who' and if an object pronoun works (*me, you, him, her, it, us* or *them*) use 'whom'. If you are still unsure then use 'who', particularly in normal speech, as using 'whom' incorrectly, as the grammar commentator David Marsh has observed, is marginally worse as not only will you be making a mistake but you will sound pompous in doing so.

Rule 12

The Proper Use of 'You and I'/'Me, Us and We'

<u>The Rule:</u> Certain pronouns can only be used to refer to the subject of the sentence and others can refer only to the object of the sentence.

Personal pronouns (*I, you, he, she, it, they, we, me, them, her, him,* and *us*) can be subdivided into two groups: pronouns that can refer to the *subject* of the sentence and pronouns that can refer to the *object* of the sentence (or clauses in complex sentences). For example:

I went to work today.

You ate all the pies!

We work well as a team.

She is my best friend.

In all of the sentences above, the pronoun is subjective (the one doing the action): *I, you, we* and *she*.

The second group of personal pronouns refer only to the object of the sentence because they are *acted upon* by the subject and the verb. For instance:

*My mother told **her** not to tell lies.*

*The students don't understand **him**.*

*Nobody takes any notice of **me**.*

Objective pronouns can only appear as the object of a sentence, words such as 'me', 'them', 'her', 'him' and 'us' ('it' and 'you' can be both subjective and objective pronouns). Most of the time it is clear if a pronoun appears in the wrong position in a sentence as it sounds uncomfortable and semi-literate: '**Her** is my best friend' or 'The students don't understand **he**'. A typical mistake and one that many people get confused about is in using 'I' and 'me' interchangeably. For example:

Michael and me are working together.

Michael and I are working together.

The second sentence is correct because the subject of the sentence is 'Michael and I' collectively, so the subjective pronoun must be used in order for the sentence to be grammatically sound. Problems occur when other agents muscle in on a sentence making it harder to distinguish who is the subject and who is the object of the sentence. For example:

The manager told Michael and me to go home.

The manager told Michael and I to go home.

The first sentence is correct because the manager is the subject of the sentence, 'Michael and me' are the object and 'I' is a subjective pronoun. If the sentence is rewritten in the passive form: 'Michael and I were told by the manager to go home' the subject and object change places and hence their corresponding pronouns must also change accordingly.

The main issue here relates to matters of linguistic register. The annual televised Christmas Day speech by Queen Elizabeth II usually contains phrases such as 'on behalf of my family and I' and this has led to the misapprehension that using 'I' in place of 'me' is more formal and therefore must always be correct. It isn't and is only correct when referring to the subject of the sentence. For example:

Our hosts threw an extravagant party on behalf of my family and I.

The sentence above sounds very formal and correct but is in fact completely wrong. It should be 'my family and me' in the object position. In everyday speech, 'me and my family' would also be correct but grammatical etiquette decrees that it is polite to place other people before yourself in lists, as if metaphorically holding the door open for them. Perhaps the last word on this should go to 1970s disco divas Sister Sledge, who were right on the money when it came to using the correct personal pronoun when they sang '*We are family, I got all my sisters with me.*'

In Summary

The subjective and objective pronoun forms are specific to their use and position in a sentence or clause. '*I,*' '*he,*' '*she,*' '*we*' and '*they*' are all subjective pronouns that can be used only in relation to the subject. '*Me,*' '*him,*' '*her,*' '*us*' and '*them*' are all objective forms. The pronouns '*you*' and '*it*' can be either subjective or objective. If in doubt when describing a pair, remove one half of the pair and see if the sentence sounds correct: 'My family and me are going on holiday/ Me is going on holiday/*I* am going on holiday/*My* family and I are going on holiday.'

English is particularly rich in adjectives due to its habit of greedily adopting and absorbing words from other languages. In simple terms, adjectives are words that describe nouns and/or pronouns. It is common to view adjectives as *describing words*, words that add colour and texture to sentences. There are however, five classes of adjective, and each performs a specific function within a sentence:

Possessive Adjectives (see possessive pronouns on page 79) such as: *my/mine, yours, his, hers, ours, theirs* and *its*.

Descriptive Adjectives such as: *beautiful, great, fantastic, big, tall.*

Numerical Adjectives are used to describe quantities and amounts of nouns. This class can be divided into three subtypes:

The **definite**, which records the exact quantity or position such as *first, second, third* or *one, two, three.*

The **indefinite**, which records inexact or general quantities such as *some, few, lots, much* and *many*.

The **distributive**, which is used to cache, collect or disperse nouns such as *each, every, other* and *another*.

Demonstrative Adjectives such as: *this, that, these* and *those* (see demonstrative pronouns on page 78).

Interrogative Adjectives are commonly referred to as question words such as *which, what* and *where*.

Comparative and Superlative Adjectives

In addition to the five classes above, some adjectives also have related comparatives and superlative forms, which are used to provide a sense of the degree to which the adjective is being ascribed. For example:

nice, nicer, nicest
*I have a **nice** car but my brother's car is **nicer** than mine. Our father's car, however, is the **nicest** of all.*

In the example above, **nice** is the *simple positive* adjective, **nicer** the *comparative* and **nicest** the *superlative* (or *ultimate*). Not all comparative and superlative forms are regular however, there are a small number of irregular adjectives that have different forms (regular adjectives form their comparatives and superlatives by adding 'er' or 'est' or by prefixing with 'most'), for example: *bad, worse, the worst* or *good, better, the best.* In contrast, there are also some positive adjectives that it is impossible to make comparatives or superlatives out of such as *dead* (something either *is* or *isn't* dead, it can't be *deader* than something else).

Rule 13

———◆———

Don't Use No Double Negatives

The Rule: Two negatives cancel each other out
to make a positive and should be avoided in
formal speech and prose.

———◆———

The use (or misuse) of double negatives is one of the rules
of English grammar that from the outset seems to be
logical and make perfect sense but so many examples of
the structure have entered into common expressions and
phrases that it becomes difficult to decide when using a
double negative is acceptable and when it is not. There are
two distinct usages of double negatives in common speech
and prose. One, it seems, is considered bad diction, and can
overcomplicate sentences, the other is a perfectly legitimate
rhetorical device regularly employed by poets, pop stars,
politicians and heavyweight boxing champions. But let's
start with the guiding principle.

In English, statements are negated in three ways, most
commonly by the addition of the adverb *not* (after verbs
such as *will, can, be, must, have* etc.) or the contracted
form *n't*. Other forms of negation occur by the addition

of adverbs and pronouns such as *never, nothing* and *nobody* and the use of prefixes like *dis, un, in/im* and *non*.

The problem, in terms of clarity, occurs when two negative forms appear in the same clause in a sentence. Consider the following scenario:

Teacher (to unruly pupil): *Could you leave the room please, your behaviour is unacceptable.*

Pupil (to teacher): *But I haven't done nothing, sir.*

The pupil's response is a classic example of a double negative construction with 'haven't' followed by 'nothing'. Following the laws of logic therefore, by not doing 'nothing', the pupil is inadvertently admitting to having done something, despite his protestations to the contrary. The pupil should have said, 'I haven't done anything, sir,' although in this situation that was probably self-evident if they had been wasting time disrupting the lesson.

So far so good, or at least it makes sense that the addition of an extra negative modifies the first negative to produce positive meaning. However, this rule is not as clear-cut as it first appears. Consider the lyrics to the following well-known pop songs:

*'We **don't** need **no** education'*
'Another Brick In The Wall', Pink Floyd

*'I **can't** get **no** satisfaction'*
'Satisfaction', The Rolling Stones

*'It's **not unusual** to be loved by anyone'*
'It's Not Unusual', Tom Jones

To strictly apply the rules of double negation to any of the famous lines above would be to ruin the sentiment or sense in the songs. Is Mick Jagger saying, for instance, that he is actually satisfied all of the time and could do with a break? Are Pink Floyd being ironic and actually saying what 'we need' is more education of the harrowing variety depicted in the song? The lines sound much flatter and nondescript if corrected to 'I can't get any satisfaction' or 'It is usual to be loved by someone'.

It isn't just in pop songs where the liberal use of double negatives seems to thrive unchecked, poets have long used the form without anybody batting an eyelid:

'By innocence I swear, And by my youth
I have one heart, one bosom, one truth,
And that no woman has; nor **never none**
Shall mistress be of it, save I alone.'

'The Friar's Tale', Geoffrey Chaucer

'Words at once true and kind, Or **not untrue**
and **not unkind**'

'Talking In Bed', Phillip Larkin

Larkin, a poet well known for his pedantry and often reactionary views, pulls off the considerable feat of writing a double double negative.

That's nothing! Spare a thought for the recipient of the following famous quote from Groucho Marx:

> *'I cannot say that I do not disagree with you.'*

Following the rule that two negatives make a positive it appears that Groucho is agreeing with the person he is addressing. However, closer inspection reveals that Groucho, a comedian celebrated for his dazzling word play, has slyly added a *third* negative, thereby converting the statement back to a negative again. Or, in short, Groucho simply doesn't agree at all.

The History Behind The Rule

The double negative, considered to be one of the great grammatical sins, nonetheless has uses in certain contexts where it is perfectly acceptable and memorable even. The reason lies in the fact that both Chaucer and Shakespeare, arguably the two greatest writers in the English language, were fond of using double negatives. In other European languages such as French and Spanish, the double negative is a common form used to add emphasis to the negation and this is probably why there are so many examples in classical literature. As the English language evolved from the Middle English period (Chaucer) through to the Early Modern period (Shakespeare) and beyond, concerted efforts were made to standardize English spelling and grammar.

One of the first objections to the use of the double negative in single clauses came from our old friend Bishop Robert Lowth (see the Introduction) who derided the form in his *A Short Introduction to English Grammar* (1762). Despite attempts to effectively outlaw the use of the double negative, it survived due to its close resemblance to 'litotes', a rhetorical device dating back to ancient Greece. Litotes is the ironic use of understatement or affirming something via its negative or opposite. For example: 'I **couldn't not** do you a favour', although somewhat inelegant, is grammatically correct and adds a nuanced meaning to the more prosaic 'I had to do you a favour'. Litotes is subtle and complex however, and rife in common speech. The expression 'not too bad' for example is a widespread response when asked about ones well-being but does that mean we aren't bad enough or we are just OK or we could be worse or we are actually in quite good health?

In Summary

The use of double negatives should be avoided, especially in written English and formal speech (although in poetry it is fine), but judicious use of litotes for irony or emphasis is perfectly acceptable.

Rule 14

When to Use 'Different To', 'Different From' or 'Different Than'

The Rule: In British English it is common practice to describe something as 'different from' something else. The form 'different than' is more prevalent in American English to describe comparatives. The form 'different to' is used more informally in general speech.

The dispute surrounding the correct preposition or conjunction to attach to the word 'different' has been raging in grammatical circles since the eighteenth century. Is something 'different from' something else or is it 'different than' or 'different to'? The traditional prescriptivism view is similar to the debate surrounding the splitting of infinitives in that it springs from the notion that Latin has a vice-like grip over English grammar. The argument promoting 'different from' as the only correct form states that 'different' shares the same Latin roots as the word 'differ', namely the

Latin verb *differre*. One thing can only be said to 'differ *from*' another, it can't be said to 'differ *than*' another so therefore something can only be different from something else. There you go! Sounds logical enough except the meaning of the words isn't quite the same even in Latin. The word 'different' actually came into English from Old French following the Norman Conquest, (albeit via Latin) and means 'to set apart'. The word *differre* in Latin has two meanings: *to differ* as in 'to disagree' or *to defer* in the legal sense, as in to postpone. So, 'different' and 'differ' aren't as close semantically as they initially appear, thus the argument for outlawing 'different than' is quite flimsy.

Statistical evidence suggests that 'different than' appears more widely in print in America than in Britain, leading to the charge that it is an Americanism infecting the purity of British English. This argument is also plain silly as 'different than' is also widely used in print in the United Kingdom. The objection against 'different to' (which statistics show, is almost exclusively used in British English) is that the preposition 'to' brings two things together when the meaning of 'different', as stated above, is to set them apart from one another. This argument has some merit as when making comparisons there is a clear distinction between to 'liken to' and to 'liken with'. In the former, 'liken to' is to describe similarities and the latter, 'liken with' is to assess possible differences. The problem is we use the preposition 'to' when we are stating preferences between two or more things:

I prefer watching cricket to watching football.

I prefer Italian cuisine to Mexican cuisine.

Thus, it seems natural when speaking informally about things we like and dislike and thereby indirectly describing their differences to say: 'This wine tastes different to that wine'.

The *Oxford English Dictionary* states that all three forms are permissible but points out that 'different than' is more prevalent in American English. Which one you use in written English is partly a matter of personal preference but there are some guidelines to help you decide:

Different From

'Different from' sounds more elegant preceding a clause that starts with a conjunction:

*The house appeared different **from how** it was when I was young.*

'Different from' is also appropriate when directly followed by a noun or pronoun:

*My sister is very different **from me**.*

Different Than

'Different than' can be used when the thing being compared is expressed by a single clause:

The weather today is different than yesterday.

'Different than' also works well when a clause follows describing an unexpected outcome or result:

The hotel was different than I had expected it to be.

Different To

Use 'different to' informally when comparing two things which are similar in form but differ in aspect as in when expressing preferences:

This wine tastes different to that wine.

Watching sport live is different to watching it on television.

In Summary

The arguments that 'different from' is the correct form are far from conclusive, particularly as 'different' isn't the same as to 'differ' and so doesn't necessarily take the same prepositions. The word 'than' is often used in comparative structures such as 'I know less than you' so it seems perfectly logical that it should be used when describing differences. 'Different to' is a more colloquial British form that is perfectly acceptable in everyday speech but perhaps should be avoided in formal writing in favour of 'different from' or 'different than'.

Rule 15

───※───

Tautology – Beware of Repeating Yourself and Saying the Same Thing Twice

<u>The Rule:</u> In contrast to their near-relation adverbs, which somewhat controversially can appear in various different positions in a sentence (see Rule 13), adjectives are usually placed before the noun that they are modifying. The exception to this general rule is when an indefinite pronoun is being modified by an adjective, words like 'something', 'someone', 'anybody', or 'anyone', in which case it is convention to place the adjective after the pronoun:

───※───

'By the pricking of my thumb,
<u>something wicked</u> this way comes.'

Macbeth, Act IV,
William Shakespeare

When adjectives appear in list form modifying the same noun or pronoun, they should be placed in a set order according to category. This order is reproduced innately by native speakers of English without a second thought (give or take the occasional lazy slip) but is something that often confuses non-native speakers, probably on account of variations in the order from language to language.

In English the order for adjectives is:

1) Opinion 2) Size 3) Age 4) Shape 5) Colour 6) Origin 7) Material 8) Purpose

So, an *ugly, big, old, round, black, Italian, cast-iron, frying* pan.

Minor deviations from this basic order are acceptable yet sound oddly cumbersome and unnatural: 'old, black, Italian, cast-iron, round, ugly, big, frying pan' is hardly a grammatical hanging offence but sounds inelegant. The listing of adjectives, other than placing them in the correct order, is problematic in other ways. The overuse of adjectives is considered to be a symptom of bad style in formal writing and, moreover, can lead to inadvertent tautology (saying the same thing twice).

Tautologies are particularly prevalent when over-egging comparative and superlative adjectives. For example, 'The most juiciest tomatoes I have ever tasted' or 'I hope to do more better in my exams this year than last year' (unlikely if the said exams are in English grammar or composition). Everyday English is littered with tautologies, chiefly due to the pernicious influence of marketing and advertising and we have become inured to seeing and hearing phrases such as 'Biggest, largest ever sale'. Marketing and advertising are also responsible for a related type of tautology known as 'pleonasm' – short phrases placed adjacent to each other that essentially mean the same thing. Think of expressions such as 'true fact' or 'pub bar' and promotional materials offering 'free gifts' or 'extra bonuses.'

The subject of tautology was raised in The Houses of Parliament during a debate on education. The Secretary of State for Education, Michael Gove, took his counterpart, Tristan Hunt to task for using the phrase 'ongoing Continuing Professional Development'. Gove ridiculed Mr Hunt for speaking in tautologies, although strictly speaking, 'ongoing continuing' is a pleonasm. The irony regarding this exchange of pedantry is that the expression 'continuing professional development' is a tautology in itself. Pleonasm can however, be used for rhetorical effect to add emphasis or to highlight a particular idea as the following example demonstrates:

> *'Let me tell you this, when social workers offer*
> *you, free, gratis and for nothing, something to*
> *hinder you from swooning, which with them is*
> *an obsession, it is useless to recoil . . .'*
>
> *Molloy*,
> Samuel Beckett

In a world that is becoming increasingly abbreviated, a form of tautology can be found in a tendency to repeat the last word of common acronyms such as ATM machine, PIN number and HIV virus.

In Summary

Follow the standard of categories when describing something (opinion, size, age, shape, colour, origin, material and purpose) but be careful not to string together too many adjectives that are synonymous with each other as this can make writing seem slack and overwrought.

The Essential Tools
The Correct Uses of the Different Forms of Punctuation

The principal punctuation marks in English are as follow:

The Full Stop or Period (US)

Used to mark the end of a sentence and in abbreviations for which there are several conventions:

1. A full stop should be placed at the end of an abbreviation when the final letter of the abbreviation doesn't correspond with the final letter of the full word. For example:

   Jesus Christ was born c. 4–6 AD

   The abbreviation for circa is '*c*' and ending in 'a' means it requires an additional full stop. In contrast 'Mr' as the standard abbreviation for 'mister' does correspond and so no additional dot is required.

2. A full stop should be placed after titles such as Cllr. and Dr. as they are formal modes of address. Some

acronyms (the initials of words that when run together can be pronounced as a word) do not require full stops as they are pronounced in speech as an entirety and not as separate letters. For example: NASA (National Aeronautics and Space Agency).

3. Certain Latin words and phrases such as *etcetera* (etc.), and *exepli gratia* (e.g.) should always be written with full stops.

The Comma (See Rule 17)

The Question Mark

The question mark is probably the easiest punctuation mark as it only has one usage; namely to denote that a sentence is a question and not a statement. The only things to remember are that a full stop is not required after a question mark and that it is considered bad style to use more than one or in combination with an exclamation mark (although this is depressingly common in emails and text messages). It is also to be noted that some sentences, although appearing to need a question mark, often don't. For example:

I wonder if it will rain today.

This is a speculative statement and not a direct question.

The Exclamation Mark

This should be used to add emphasis in the sense of an expression of surprise or incredulity, or as an expression of extreme emotion. Exclamation marks should be used fairly sparingly and, like the question mark, shouldn't be used in multiples. There is a modern 'fashion' for using them in a faux ironic manner to express disdain or cynicism, but this is very much a product of modern electronic communication.

The Colon (See Rule 17)

The Semicolon (See Rule 17)

The Apostrophe (See Rule 16)

Inverted Commas (or Quotation Marks/ Speech Marks)

Inverted commas are used to denote either direct speech or direct quotations form other sources or texts. In the United Kingdom, single inverted 'commas' are common. In the United States double inverted commas are more prevalent than single ones.

There are some conventions for using other forms of punctuation inside quotation marks, which are as follows:

Full stops and commas always go inside quotation marks when quoting from other sources (by way of consistency), or in simple direct speech:

> *'If I hear that song one more time, I'll scream,' said Polly.*

> *Rose said, 'If I hear that song one more time, I'll scream.'*

When there is a question outside of the source material to be quoted and inside quoted material, only one question mark is required and should be placed inside the quotation mark (or marks):

> *'Did they ask, "Why did you do that?"'*

In the example above, the quote within the quote is placed in double quotes quote within single quotes.

Parentheses

Parentheses are used for additional material or clarification that is subordinate to the main information in the sentence. In this sense they can function as an aside in the similar way that bracketing commas function (see Rule 17). Parenthesis can also contain further items of clarification such as dates or the expanded form of abbreviations or acronyms.

Hyphens

Hyphens are used to join two or more words to create a compound adjective used to describe a noun. Compound adjectives are made up of a noun and an adjective, or a noun and a participle, or an adjective and a participle. Compounds such as *bad-tempered, quick-thinking, good-looking, chocolate-covered* or *user-generated* need to be hyphenated if they are attributive (preceding the word that they modify). For example:

*She served up some **chocolate-covered strawberries** for dessert.*

The hyphen shouldn't be used if the noun object is in the subject position in the sentence. For example:

The strawberries she served for dessert were chocolate covered.

Hyphens are also used with compound numbers, such as twenty-one, thirty-three etc. up to ninety-nine.

Hyphens are also used with certain prefixes such as 'ex-' (as in former), 'self-' , and 'all-' : 'ex-boyfriend', 'self-assured', 'all-inclusive'.

Rule 16

— ❧ —

How to Use Apostrophes Correctly

The Rule: **The apostrophe has three uses: to form possessives of nouns, to show the omission of letters in contracted word forms and in rare instances to indicate plural forms of letters.**

— ❧ —

The use of what is often referred to as 'The Grocer's Apostrophe' is considered to be one of the great grammatical howlers. Signs outside high street shops regularly advertise 'Apple's Half Price' or 'Key's Cut While U Wait'. A chain of coffee shops aptly named 'Apostrophe' were recently in the news for using the advertising motto: 'Great taste on it's way'. The reverse is also true in situations where apostrophes have been left out: 'This Weeks Special Offer'.

I have a confession to make. As someone who had their post-graduate thesis returned from the external examiner on the grounds that it contained: 'The worst case of apostrophe blindness I have ever encountered'; I have some sympathy for the perpetrators of these mistakes. Over the years I've made a conscious effort to get to grips with the apostrophe but still have to take care and double check. The rules governing the use of apostrophes are actually quite straightforward so why do so many people struggle with them? The reason is confusing the two main uses of apostrophes: the formation of possessives and indicating the omission of letters in contracted forms.

1. Apostrophes are used to show the possessive form of singular nouns and this formed by adding **'s** after the noun:

David Beckham's haircut.

Philip Larkin's poetry.

Manchester United's new manager.

This also holds true if the singular noun ends in an 's':

Davy Jones's haircut

Ted Hughes's poetry

The confusion starts to creep in when using apostrophes to show the possessive form of plural nouns. Regular plural nouns end in 's' or 'es' and their possessive is formed by placing the apostrophe after the 's' and not adding an extra 's':

My horses' stables. (The stables belongs to my horses)

The girls' bedrooms. (The bedrooms belong to the girls)

The students' house. (More than one student lives there)

The problem with the last example is that 'the student's' house would be correct if only one student lived in/owned the house in question. If the plural noun is irregular then the possessive takes the same form as the singular – add an apostrophe and 's'. For example:

The children's playhouse.

The women's institute.

It seems then that the use of errant apostrophes stems from the mistaken belief that plural nouns are formed by adding an apostrophe and 's' when only the possessive form of irregular plurals are formed in this way.

2. The second main use of apostrophes is to show the omission of letters in contracted forms. Below are the contractions that cause the most problems:

'I'm' (I am); 'you're' (you are);'he's' (he is); 'she's' (she is); it's (it is); 'we're' (we are); they're (they are) and 'who's' (who is)

The possessive pronouns: 'Yours', 'his', 'hers', 'its', 'ours', 'theirs' etc. do not require apostrophes to denote possession because they already function as possessives. This leads to another common apostrophe gaff, namely confusing the possessive pronoun 'its' with the contraction 'it is' (as in the error by the Apostrophe café chain). Similarly there can be confusion over the use of 'whose' and 'who's'. For example:

Who's that girl sitting over there?

Whose line is it anyway?

The trick here, if unsure, is to expand the contractions and see if the sentence still makes sense: '**Who is** line is it anyway?'

As ever with English grammar, there is an exception to the rule about possessive pronouns. It is correct to use apostrophes with certain indefinite pronouns such as 'somebody' or 'anybody':

Is this somebody's coat?

It's anybody's guess who it belongs to.

Other Uses of Apostrophes

When two or more singular nouns possess the same thing, add an apostrophe plus 's' to the last noun listed:

I'm going round to Michael and Jane's house tonight.

When two or more singular nouns are listed but possess something individually, add an apostrophe to each unit in the list:

I will mark Michael's and Jane's exam papers tonight.

Apostrophes shouldn't be used with dates and periods of time unless referring to something that 'belongs' unequivocally to the time frame:

In the 1980s, there was a lot of innovation in music technology.

The music of the 1980's was very innovative.

On rare occasions it is permissible to use apostrophes to form plurals of letters that are used in colloquial expressions such as: 'mind your P's and Q's.'. The form 'Ps and Qs' is more common.

In Summary

Use apostrophe and 's' after all singular nouns
to denote possession. With regular plural nouns
omit the additional 's' and place the apostrophe
at the end of the word. With irregular plurals,
form with the apostrophe and 's'. Never use
apostrophes to form plural nouns (*apple's* and
pear's etc.) and never use apostrophes with
possessive pronouns (pay particular attention to
its/it's and *whose/who's*).

Rule 17

Uses and Abuses of Commas, Colons and Semicolons

<u>The Rule:</u> Commas are used to separate clauses, after introductory phrases, in lists, in place of conjunctions and after phrases of direct address. Colons are used to introduce listed items, direct speech, quotations, examples and explanations. Semicolons are used to connect two or more related main clauses, in complex lists and with conjunctive adverbs and transitional phrases such as 'however', or 'therefore'.

The Main Uses of Commas

The comma is perhaps the most important punctuation mark in relation to its correct or incorrect usage for, as discussed in Rule 10, putting commas in the wrong place can alter the meaning or essential sense of a sentence. Commas arc used to separate independent clauses. For example:

The show was over, but none of the audience wanted to leave.

Today is our anniversary, so I'm taking my wife out to dinner.

In the examples above, the comma is followed by a coordinating conjunction. The seven coordinating conjunctions (words that join main clauses in order to give equal emphasis to both parts of a sentence) are: 'for', 'and', 'nor', 'but', 'or', 'yet' and 'so'. A simple way to remember the seven coordinating conjunctions is by the acronym FANBOYS. Commas should always be followed by coordinating conjunctions between clauses of equal importance.

Commas are also used with words, phrases, or clauses that come before the main clause:

While I was sleeping, the dog soiled the carpet.

If you are sick, you should to see doctor.

There are certain other words that should be followed by a comma at the start of sentences such as 'yes', 'however', 'nonetheless' and 'well'. For example:

Yes, I'd like to come to your party.

Nonetheless, the match went ahead despite the bad weather.

A bracketing comma is the term used to describe commas that separate non-defining (or non-restrictive) clauses in a sentence. This clause adds non-essential information to the sentence and functions as an aside to the main clause or clauses. For example:

Jane and David, two colleagues from work, are coming to dinner next week.

The simple trick to test the use of bracketing commas is if the clause they contain can be removed without any loss of meaning to the main clause:

Jane and David are coming to dinner next week.

Bracketing commas can cause ambiguity if they are used in error to separate essential information in a sentence:

Footballers, who dive, are cheats.

This sentence suggests that all footballers dive and therefore all of them are cheats, whereas if the bracketing commas are removed, only the 'footballers who dive are cheats.'

The Oxford Comma

Commas are also used when describing lists of three or more constituent parts. For example: 'I like eating Spanish, Italian, and French cuisine.' The addition of a comma after 'Italian' is an example of usage of the Oxford comma – so called as it is the standard of the Oxford University Press. The convention for using the Oxford comma is more prevalent in American English (where it is also known as The Harvard Comma) but has its detractors who argue it is unnecessary. In some instances, however, omitting the comma before the 'and' can cause ambiguity. Consider the following acceptance speech at an academy awards ceremony from a gushing actor:

I dedicate this Oscar to my parents,
the director and the producer.

Now the actor's parents may well have been the director and the producer of course, such is the prevalence of nepotism in Hollywood, but the convention of thanking everyone possible suggests that they aren't. Similarly, the preacher who exhorts his congregation with the sentence: 'Praise be to my brother and sister, Jesus Christ and The Virgin Mary'; although possibly speaking figuratively, isn't intending to suggest the last two names on his list are his actual siblings.

In truth, such minor semantic ambiguities are rare so the use or non-use of the Oxford comma is more a matter of personal preference. Newspaper journalists and print style guides, particularly in the United Kingdom tend to discourage the addition of a comma before the 'and' to save space and in the interests of brevity. Some sympathy should be shown towards the unfortunate sub-editor on *The Times* for the following classic blunder, when previewing a Peter Ustinov documentary for the television listings page:

> *By train, plane and sedan chair, Peter Ustinov retraces a journey made by Mark Twain a century ago. The highlights of his global tour include encounters with Nelson Mandela, an 800-year-old demigod and a dildo collector.*

Other Uses of Commas

Commas are used in citing the names of geographical locations, items in dates (except the month and day), addresses and official titles. For example:

> *I was born in Brighton, England, on 10 December 1968, at 4 a.m. My full name is Joseph Algernon Swinburn Piercy, The King of All of The Belgians, of 32, Soggy Bottom Lane, Ghent, Belgium.*

Commas are used to switch between speech and the narrative or main discourse:

'She turned towards him, "I don't think that will be necessary," she said dismissively.'

Commas are also used when directly addressing a person or persons:

'Ladies and Gentlemen, please be upstanding for the bride and groom.'

The Main Uses of Colons

A colon should be used to introduce direct speech and quotations (placed inside inverted commas). Colons are also used to introduce illustrative examples relating to the preceding statement or to introduce lists or items. For example:

Eric Cantona had a successful career as a footballer in France and England playing for the following teams: Auxerre, Marseille, Leeds and Manchester United.

The Main Uses of Semicolons

Semicolons are tricky as they appear, on the surface, to separate clauses. The semicolon confuses. There is an argument that they are unnecessary and are just writers being 'showy'. The anti-semicolon brigade also point out, with some justification, that few people actually bother to use them, and when they do they use them incorrectly. The simple explanation of their usage is that semicolons separate two main clauses that are closely related to each other, either by subject or aspect or theme. The test is that a sentence containing a semicolon can be split into two separate, coherent sentences; although, for reasons of style and fluidity, (or not reading like a robot in a science fiction film), the writer has chosen not to do so. Some writers, particularly ones who have an ear for the natural rhythm and cadence of words, love a semicolon; others avoid them like the plague. The following example from the novel *The Gift* by Vladimir Nabokov displays subtle mastery of the semicolon:

> *'The woman, thickset and no longer young, with bow-legs and a rather attractive pseudo-Chinese face, wore an astrakhan jacket; the wind, having rounded her, brought a whiff of rather good but slightly stale perfume.'*

There, in a nutshell, is a very adroit description in a single sentence, vivid and full of judicious details. The writer clearly wanted to add a further sensual perception to his description that could have been clunky if he'd just written: 'She smelled of stale perfume'.

Artistry aside, however, there are situations when a semicolon should be used in favour of a comma. Semicolons should always be used with conjunctive adverbs (e.g. 'consequently') if the adverb or adverbial phrase (also called a transitional phrase) is being used to join two related independent clauses. This is particularly true with cause and effect situations:

I worked really hard to try and get a new contract; consequently, I've been rewarded with a promotion.

My alarm failed to go off again; subsequently, I was late for work and got the sack.

The rule here is that the use of a conjunctive adverb or transitional phrase such as 'in comparison with' or 'on the other hand' should be preceded by a semicolon and not a comma.

Here is a list of conjunctive adverbs and transitional phrases that should take a semicolon, unless the sentence begins with a word such as 'however', or 'furthermore' and then a comma is required:

accordingly	furthermore	next
additionally	hence	nonetheless
again	henceforth	notably
almost	however	now
although	in addition	on the other hand
anyway	in comparison	otherwise
as a result	in contrast	rather
besides	in fact	similarly
certainly	incidentally	still
comparatively	indeed	subsequently
consequently	instead	that is
contrarily	just as	then
conversely	likewise	thereafter
elsewhere	meanwhile	therefore
equally	moreover	thus
eventually	namely	undoubtedly
finally	nevertheless	uniquely
further (to)		

Other Uses of Semicolons

Semicolons should also be used when additional defining information is included in lists, primarily to avoid overuse of the comma and separate each constituent part. Think, for example, about a list of the original line up of The Rolling Stones:

The band consisted of Brian Jones, guitarist and harmonica player; Ian Stewart, pianist; Mick Jagger, lead vocalist; Keith Richards, guitarist; Bill Wyman, bassist; and Charlie Watts on the drums.

The *Point Virgule* is Dead, Long Live the *Point Virgule*!

The declining use of the semicolon has been a matter of some debate since the mid-twentieth century: is it really necessary? The argument stems from the fact that the semicolon's appearance in printed materials has radically declined over the last hundred or so years. Is this because modern writers are unsure of how to use the semicolon correctly? If so, they seem to be getting along OK without it and are able to use a combination of colons or commas instead of semicolons without anybody noticing the difference.

The debate is particularly virulent in France where the anti-semicolon lobby, including the writer Philippe Djian (author of the novel *37°2 le matin* – better known in English as *Betty Blue*), view the *point virgule* (to give the semicolon its French name), as an example of an Anglicism that has infected the purity of the French language. In order to protect French, the *point virgule* must die! On the other side of the fence, several prominent French academics have pointed out that writers from the classical French canon, such as Victor Hugo, Gustav Flaubert and Marcel Proust, were all ardent users of the *point virgule* in their prose. Below are some quotes from prominent English language writers on the subject of the semicolon and whether or not they are strictly necessary:

'Not many people use it much any more, do they? Should it be used more? I think so, yes. A semicolon is a partial pause, a different way of pausing, without using a full stop. I use it all the time.'

Beryl Bainbridge

'With educated people, I suppose, punctuation is a matter of rule; with me it is a matter of feeling. But I must say I have a great respect for the semicolon; it's a useful little chap.'

President Abraham Lincoln

'You practically do not use semicolons at all.
This is a symptom of mental defectiveness,
probably induced by camp life.'

George Bernard Shaw (in a letter to T.E.
Lawrence about Lawrence's autobiography,
The Seven Pillars of Wisdom.)

'Do not use semicolons. They are transvestite
hermaphrodites, standing for absolutely nothing.
All they do is show you've been to college.'

Kurt Vonnegut

'Did you know by the way that this book
['Coming Up for Air'] hasn't got a semicolon in
it? I decided about that time that the semicolon
is an unnecessary stop and that I would write
my next book without one.'

George Orwell in a letter to his editor at Secker &
Warburg

In Summary

Care should be taken to place commas correctly
in sentences as misplacing them can scramble
the meaning of the sentence or cause ambiguity.
Use the test of removing independent clauses
encapsulated within bracketing commas to
see if the sentence still makes sense. Colons
should be preceded by an independent clause
or introductory phrase. Semicolons should be
used when two or more related main clauses
(that could stand alone as sentences) are joined
to add greater clarity and purpose to a sentence,
and should precede the use of conjoining
adjectives between clauses (words such as
'subsequently', 'moreover' etc.)

The Essential Tools
Advanced Grammar

The following two rules are interesting inasmuch as they actually aren't rules at all, people just think that they are. This may beggar the question: why include rules that aren't rules in a book about essential grammatical rules? The reason is that the belief in them is so widespread, it is important to be able to recognize the need to be flexible with grammar. As we have seen with split infinitives and the debate surrounding 'different from' and 'different than', it is useful to know the background to be able to make an informed choice.

Rule 18 and Rule 19 relate to the positioning of prepositions and conjunctions in sentences and so by way of introduction it will be useful to briefly outline the function of both parts of speech.

Prepositions

A **preposition** links nouns, pronouns and phrases to other words in a sentence. The word or phrase that the preposition introduces is called the object of the preposition.

A preposition usually indicates the temporal, spatial or logical relationship of its object to the rest of the sentence as in the following examples:

*The book is **on** the table.*

*The book is **beneath** the table.*

*The book is leaning **against** the table.*

*The book is **beside** the table.*

*She held the book **over** the table.*

*She read the book **during** class.*

In each of the examples, a preposition locates the noun 'book' in space or in time. Put simply, it is the (pre) *position* of the object/noun.

A prepositional phrase is made up of the preposition, its object and any associated adjectives or adverbs. A prepositional phrase can function as a noun, an adjective, or an adverb. The most common prepositions are: *about, above, across, after, against, along, among, around, at, before, behind, below, beneath, beside, between, beyond, but, by, despite, down, during, except, for, from, in, inside, into, like, near, of, off, on, onto, out, outside, over, past, since, through, throughout, till, to, toward, under, underneath, until, up, upon, with, within,* and *without.*

Conjunctions

A conjunction is a word that 'joins'. A conjunction connects two parts of a sentence or separate phrases within a sentence together. Conjunctions fall into two groups: coordinating conjunctions (*and, but, or, nor, for, yet, so*) and subordinating conjunctions (*although, because, since, unless* etc.).

Conjunctions have three aspects: form, function and position.

1. The three forms:
a) Single words: 'and', 'but' or 'although'.
b) Compound forms and phrases that often end in 'as' or 'that': 'as long as' etc.
c) Correlative forms: pairs of words matching conjunctions with adverbs to form phrases like 'not only . . . but also'.

2. The two main functions:
a) Coordinating conjunctions are used to join two parts of a sentence that are grammatically equal. The two parts may be single words or clauses, for example:

Jack and Jill went up the hill.

The water was warm, but I didn't go swimming.

b) Subordinating conjunctions are used to join a subordinate dependent clause to a main clause, for example:

Although it was cold, I went swimming.

3. Conjunctions occupy two positions depending on type:

a) Coordinating conjunctions always come between the words or clauses that they join.

b) Subordinating conjunctions usually come at the beginning of the dependent (subordinate) clause.

Rule 18

Ending Sentences with Prepositions Can Bring You Down

The Rule: Prepositions should not be left dangling at the end of sentences or clauses but should always be placed before the word (prepositional object) to which they are related.

The History Behind the Rule

The term 'preposition' is derived from the Latin *prae*, meaning 'before' and *ponere,* meaning *'to place'.* In Latin, the preposition always goes **before** the prepositional object that is linked to and is never placed after it. This rule has led to the assumption that prepositions in English should never be placed after their objects and especially not at the end of sentences.

The first known objection to so called 'dangling preposition' is believed to have been the poet and playwright John Dryden who wrote a critique of Ben Jonson. In Dryden's eyes it was a flaw in Jonson's style to place prepositions at the end of clauses. Bishop Robert Lowth (see Introduction) endorsed Dryden's position in his 1762 book, *A Short Introduction to English Grammar* and was further supported by Victorian grammarian Henry Alford in *A Plea for the Queen's English* (1864).

As with other contentious areas of English grammar, the prohibition against ending sentences or clauses with 'dangling prepositions' hinges on forcing Latin grammar on to English.

Exceptions to the Rule

In simple sentences prepositions usually go before their object:

*She has fallen **off** the **wagon**.*

*Will you write **to me**?*

There are nonetheless certain circumstances whereby slavishly sticking to Bishop Lowth's (and others) dictum can make things rather awkward. There are four linguistic structures and situations in which it sounds more natural to end a sentence or clause with a preposition:

1. **Using Phrasal Verbs in Simple Sentences**

   Phrasal verbs are everyday, colloquial expressions formed with a verb and preposition. Often the same combination can have multiple meanings depending on context:

   I have broken up with my girlfriend.

   When does college break up for summer?

   She broke up a fight between two friends last night.

   Consider instruction manuals for electrical devices:

   When not in use the computer should always be switched off.

   Rewrite the sentence without the preposition at the end and it sounds like Yoda from the *Star Wars* films:

   When not in use switched off the computer should always be.

   OK, so the sentence can be rewritten as 'The computer should always be switched off when not in use', which is probably the most elegant solution, but we would use the first sentence in standard speech without worrying too much about being misunderstood or thinking we'd made a serious blunder. However, as the following examples illustrate, it is often impossible not to leave the preposition at the end of the sentence when using idiomatic expressions (unless impersonating an 800-year-old Jedi from the planet Dagobah):

He does go on; The children are playing up; She likes being taken out.

Go on he does; Playing up the children are; Being taken out she likes.

2. **At the End of Relative Clauses**
   When phrasal verbs are used in complex sentences it is often quite normal to find them placed at the end of sentences. For example:

   *He should understand the big responsibility that he is taking **on**.*

   *I have just finished the new proposal that you will be looking **at**.*

3. **In Simple Sentences Using Infinitives**
   For example:

   I had nobody to talk to.

   There wasn't anybody I wanted to sit with.

If the second sentence is rewritten as: 'There wasn't any-body with which I wanted to sit', it sounds fussy and overly mannered.

4. **Question Forms**

When Diana Ross sang *'Do you know where you're going to?'* it sounded perfectly natural and would have sounded very strange if she had sung *'Do you know to where you are going?'* Many simple question forms with 'who', 'what', 'where' etc. end with prepositions and sound perfectly natural: 'What films are you interested in?' or 'In what films are you interested?' I know which question I'd be more interested in answering.

This is the Kind of Arrant Pedantry Up With Which I Will Not Put

There is a famous story about Winston Churchill concerning the use of prepositions. At some point during the early years of the Second World War, Churchill was preparing one of his celebrated speeches to be broadcast over the radio and circulated a draft to civil service clerks to check over for grammatical accuracy. When one of the copies returned with a sentence rearranged because it ended in a preposition, Churchill is said to have issued an irate memo stating: 'This is the kind of arrant pedantry up with which I will not put.' The anecdote has appeared in various newspapers, books and magazines over the years and, although now generally considered to be apocryphal, it succinctly demonstrates the problems that can occur by sticking too strictly to a 'rule'.

In Summary

The rule that prepositions should not be placed at the end of sentences is a classic grammar myth as there are lots of circumstances where it is more natural and often correct to do so. Nonetheless, it is advisable to explore other sentence structures, particularly in formal writing, to see if there is an elegant alternative as too many dangling prepositions in a text can sometimes appear slapdash.

Rule 19

And Avoid Starting Sentences with Conjunctions

<u>The Rule:</u> It is considered bad style to start sentences with conjunctions such as 'and', 'but', 'with' etc. as their primary function is to join words and clauses within a sentence.

But is it a Rule?

The rule that you shouldn't start sentences with conjunctions, particularly 'and' or 'but' appears to have no historical precedent at all. It is, however, one of the few rules that almost everyone can remember being taught in English composition classes. This has led to the theory put forward by some linguists, most notably David Marsh and Arnold Zwicky, that 'the rule' as it stands is an invention of the formal education system.

There isn't any reason at all why sentences can't be started with coordinating conjunctions, other than it is quite difficult to do effectively without making a bit of a mess of things. This is taken as the reason why English teachers encourage young learners that it is wrong to begin sentences with coordinating conjunctions (FANBOYS – see Rule 17). With practice and some thought, however, it can be a useful rhetorical device. For example:

> *'For her to reach her full potential she must concentrate for longer periods. With all due respect sir, I find your haircut offensive.'And death shall have no dominion.'*

> Dylan Thomas

The last example above is from a poem, admittedly, and starting sentences with conjunctions in poetry is common practice:

> *'And other withered stumps of time Were told upon the walls; staring forms Leaned out, leaning, hushing the room enclosed.'*

> **'The Wasteland'**, T. S. Eliot

And it isn't just in poetry, however, that skilful or powerful sentences are constructed with a preposition at the start. The traditional wedding vows from *The Common Book Of Prayer* (1549) cites the following ceremonial virtues:

> *'With this Ring I thee wed.'*
> *'With my body I thee worship.'*
> *'And with all my worldly goods I thee endow.'*

Similarly, the King James Bible (1611) is littered with sentences that begin with conjunctions, usually 'And' but also 'So' and 'Yet'. So prevalent, in fact, is this stylistic signature, it is rare to find a sentence that doesn't start with a conjunction:

> *'In the beginning God created the heaven and the earth. And the earth was without form, and void; and darkness was upon the face of the deep. And the Spirit of God moved upon the face of the waters. And God said, Let there be light: and there was light. And God saw the light, that it was good: and God divided the light from the darkness.'*
>
> Genesis, the **King James Bible**

It seems strange, therefore, that this rule about conjunctions should ever have come about, given that historical evidence shows some of the most important texts in the history of the English language contain sentences beginning with conjunctions. It seems entirely plausible that modern linguists and language critics are correct in surmising that it is something that has sprung out of education. This makes sense because the main function of conjunctions is to join words and clauses and it may cause confusion to teach young learners other ways they can be used.

Because I Said So!

It is considered to be entirely appropriate to start sentences with subordinating conjunctions such as 'although' and 'moreover' but there is general exception to using 'because'. For example:

I didn't arrive on time because the train was late.

Because the train was late I didn't arrive on time.

The second sentence is deemed to be inelegant as it is putting the subordinate clause ('the train was late') before the main clause ('I didn't arrive on time').

'Because' is used in speech to answer short questions as in the exasperated teacher explaining to a student why he can't use 'because' at the start of sentences:

Because I said so!

'Because' has however, been used for stylistic effect at the start of sentences by poets and songwriters, most notably T.S. Eliot (again) and The Beatles:

> *'Because I do not hope to turn again*
> *Because I do not hope*
> *Because I do not hope to turn.'*

> **'Ash Wednesday'**, T.S. Eliot

148

'Because the sky is blue, it makes me cry.
Because the sky is blue, ah, ah, ah, ah.'

'Because', The Beatles

In Summary

There is no 'rule' against starting sentences with conjunctions such as 'and' or 'but' or 'with' other than it is quite tricky to do effectively. Be mindful that short sentences should be used for emphasis and effect. And writing down one idea. And adding another idea. But not linking them. And adding another idea . . . The writing quickly becomes stilted and monotonous. So, it isn't grammatically incorrect to start sentences with conjunctions (as I have been doing a lot in this section), but variety of sentence structures makes for more dynamic and readable prose.

Rule 20

❖

Pronouns Must Always be Agreeable

The Rule: Pronouns are often used to refer to somebody or something mentioned previously in the sentence (or paragraph) and this is known as its antecedent. The choice of pronoun must correspond (or 'agree') with its antecedent according to person, number (singular or plural) and gender.

❖

Matching the correct pronoun with its antecedent is usually quite straightforward with singular and plural forms.

A singular antecedent agrees with a singular pronoun:

The dog wagged its tail = dog (singular antecedent) + its (singular pronoun).

A plural antecedent agrees with a plural pronoun:

The kittens cried all night for their mother = kittens (plural antecedent) + their (plural pronoun).

So far so good but things become a little more cloudy when dealing with indefinite pronouns such as 'anyone', 'anybody', 'everyone', 'everybody', 'someone', 'somebody', 'no one', and 'nobody'. Indefinite pronouns are considered to be singular because they refer to a single collective unit. This is sometimes puzzling to people who feel that 'everyone' and 'everybody' refer to more than one person. When Nile Rogers and Bernard Edwards of the band Chic wrote their dance floor classic 'Everybody Dance' however, they were talking to everyone who heard the song hence: 'Everybody (antecedent) dance, clap your (singular pronoun) hands, clap your (singular pronoun) hands.'

This would seem, although a little perplexing, fairly easy to grasp as long as you remember that indefinite pronouns are singular. However, it is not uncommon to come across sentences such as:

Somebody has left their keys behind.

Has anybody got their phone with them?

Nobody in their right mind would do that!

The problem here is that all of the antecedents are indefinite pronouns but they are in agreement with the plural pronoun 'their'. The old-fashioned and politically incorrect solution to this problem was to use 'his' in place of their, regardless of gender. The modern solution would be to rewrite sentences as 'Nobody in his or her right mind would do that' and although this is fine, the 'his or her' breaks the flow of the sentence. The use of 'their' as gender non-specific is acceptable in situations where the singular noun does not specify an individual but can be replaced with a plural pronoun.

Identifying the antecedent and ensuring it is in agreement with the correct pronoun becomes more difficult in sentences where the pronoun may refer to more than one person. For example:

Polly told her mother that her trousers were too tight.

The ambiguity here is the question of who is wearing the tight trousers: Polly or her mother? Pronouns should always refer to the antecedent nearest to the pronoun. So in this case it is the child being somewhat impertinent about her mother's dress sense as the antecedent 'mother' is closest to the pronoun 'her.'

Multiple antecedents can cause all sorts of problems in sloppily written sentences. For example:

When Joanna backed her car into a concrete post, she badly damaged it.

Following the convention that the pronoun 'it' should refer to the nearest possible antecedent (noun or pronoun) it should be the concrete post that got badly damaged. Logic suggests however, that it was Joanna's car that probably came off worse from the encounter. Some judicious rearrangement can correct the problem:

Joanna's car got badly damaged when she backed it into a concrete post.

Although the pronoun is still closer to the concrete post than the car, the sentence makes more explicit that the pronoun 'it' refers to Joanna's car.

In Summary

In general, ensure that singular antecedents link with singular pronouns and plural antecedents with plural pronouns. The exception is when indefinite pronouns such as 'somebody' or 'anybody' are used in gender non-specific circumstances or does not specify an individual.

Rule 21

How to Spot Misplaced Correlatives

The Rule: Correlative conjunctions are pairs of words/phrases that connect and balance grammatical items (nouns, verbs, pronouns etc.). Both elements must be followed by the same part of speech or an independent clause.

Correlative conjunctions are the compound phrases: 'both . . . and'; 'not only . . . but also' and 'either . . . or/ neither . . . nor' (see Rule 8). They are used to highlight the connection between two parts of a sentence, hence, create a correlation. In order for the sentence not to appear clunky it has to be well balanced and parallel. Consider the sentence below and determine if it is properly balanced:

I not only was tired but hungry.

At first glance this appears to be OK, but read it back a few times and it starts to sound a little strange. Here is why: if you are going to use correlative conjunctions you must use both parts of the pairing in the same sentence unit. Think in terms of a set of scales with one half of the sentence being weighed against the other half. In this case the 'also' is absent from the second part of the sentence, which has tipped the balance towards the first half.

The 'not only' part of the pairing is followed by the verb 'to be' and the adjective 'tired', whereas the second part is followed by the adjective 'hungry', so again the sentence scales lurch towards the first part of the sentence.

The words following each part of the pairing do not correlate (match) as 'was' is a verb and 'hungry' is an adjective.

The sentence could be rewritten as: 'I not only was hungry but also was tired' and it would balance but still sounds a little clunky as the verb comes after the correlative conjunctions, so although it balances the sentence scales they are wobbling a little still. The most elegant solution in this case is to restrict the parts of speech being correlated down to a single item, in this case the adjectives 'tired' and 'hungry' by placing the verb before the correlating conjunction:

I was not only tired but also hungry.

The sentence is now balanced and therefore has a parallel structure.

Achieving parallel structures in sentences with correlating conjunctions becomes more difficult the more complex the sentence is. For example:

Lionel Messi not only scored the first goal but also won the penalty.

The sentence above balances two independent clauses; as with single parts of speech following correlative conjunctions, the clauses should be of comparative weight.

Correlative conjunctions can also be used to connect two antecedents and this entails the following convention for pronoun agreement (see Rule 20):

1. *Not only Polly but also the cousins showed their disappointment when Granny served up fish pie for supper.*

2. *Not only the cousins but also Polly showed her disappointment when Granny served up fish pie for supper.*

Of the two connected antecedents the second one is important in terms of agreeing with the correct pronoun. In sentence one, 'cousins' is plural therefore the pronoun 'their' is plural. In sentence two, 'Polly' is singular and so 'her' is the correct pronoun.

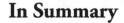

In Summary

Correlative conjunctions are not only hard to understand but also difficult to use. Be careful when using them as it is very easy to unbalance sentences without even noticing, so make sure if joining main clauses that each clause is of roughly equal length and the words following the conjunctions match. The main point to remember is to make sure that both parts of the pairing are present:

He has not only a villa in Italy but a villa in Spain. (Incorrect)

He has not only a villa in Italy __but also__ a villa in Spain. (Correct)

Rule 22

The Differences Between the Four Grammatical Cases in English

The Rule: There are four cases in the modern English language: nominative, accusative, genitive and dative. Cases relate only to nouns and pronouns and their function within a sentence.

The subtitle of this rule is 'know your cases'. It isn't that essential to know your cases in Modern English as much of the complicated inflection (words changing form and meaning according to their referents) that existed in Olde English has disappeared. We now have use of four cases: nominative, genitive, accusative, and dative. Olde English had five plus many other complicated inflections, but as the English language has evolved it has become more simple to use and understand.

The case of a noun or pronoun is *determined by what the word does in the sentence*. A noun or pronoun is in the

nominative case when it is the subject of a sentence. In the sentence, 'I am alive', 'I' is nominative because it is the subject and is also related to the verb 'to be'. The **genitive** case is mostly used for showing possession such as: 'My house' or 'The edge of the cliff.' Nouns in the genitive case are often formed by adding a possessive apostrophe or placing the word 'of' before the noun as in 'the hair of the dog.' The **accusative** case relates to nouns' or pronouns' relationship to transitive verbs in sentences, or when nouns or pronouns are the object of prepositions. For example:

Freddie Starr ate my hamster.

Go home with him.

In the first sentence, 'my hamster' is the direct object of the verb and so is in the accusative case. The sentence is taken from a notorious British tabloid newspaper headline and is accusative in more than one sense. In the second sentence, 'with him' is in the accusative sense as it is preceded by the preposition 'with'. A noun or pronoun is in the **dative** case when it is used as an indirect object. In sentences that contain both a direct and an indirect object you can distinguish between them with the following test:

I gave you the grammar book.

First find the verb in the sentence ('gave'). Then ask the question 'gave what?' to find the direct object of the verb ('the grammar book'). This only leaves the personal pronoun 'you', which must be the indirect object. Or another way to spot the indirect object is that it is always placed between the verb and the direct object:

She sent her boyfriend some flowers.

Verb = sent; Sent what? = flowers (direct object); her boyfriend = indirect object in the dative case.

In Summary

As discussed in the introduction, formal grammar of this type isn't taught in schools in this way any more. In this sense it is entirely possible to go through life never having to fret about the difference between the accusative case and the objective case (in case you were wondering, they are the same thing). There is an argument that it is useful to have at least a basic grasp of the different cases as this can be a great help when studying foreign languages, particularly if the language in question has heavily inflected forms. Should anybody ever ask for an example of a noun in the accusative case, quote the following joke by Groucho Marx:

Time flies like an arrow. Fruit flies like a banana.

Rule 23

———— ❧ ————

Be Careful What You Wish For in the Subjunctive Mood

The Rule: The subjunctive is the term given to a particular series of verb forms that were traditionally known as 'moods'. In essence, the subjunctive is used to describe *unreal* situations; to predict the potential outcome of future events; to speculate on the possible outcome of past events, or to suggest, request or demand a particular course of action.

———— ❧ ————

The term 'subjunctive' is misleading. It gives the impression of being something very highbrow and mysterious and difficult to grasp. It is actually a form that is used all the time in social interaction. The finer points of the grammatical structures will be explained below but first we need to grasp the concept.

The **subjunctive** is used to describe things that haven't happened, either in the past, the present or the future. Therefore, it can't be adequately described by normal tense structures as this event or situation has no referable time frame. Let's start with the past:

'I would have got away with it, if it weren't for you meddling kids.'

A very familiar refrain from the denouement of every episode of the cartoon series *Scooby Doo*, the sentence above is a perfect example of the past subjunctive. The villain 'didn't get away with it' and quite possibly wouldn't have regardless of the 'meddling kids'. It is an expression of an outcome that never did or possibly can never happen.

The curious thing about the subjunctive is that it mixes up tenses in the same sentence. Take another look: 'have got' (present perfect) + 'were' (the past tense of 'to be'). This is because in the past subjunctive the verb 'to be' is always expressed as 'were' regardless of other considerations.

If I were you I wouldn't have done that.

If I were you I would have gone for it.

The **past subjunctive** is used to describe what may be termed 'contrary to fact' (as in, 'didn't happen') or hypothetical situations. These sentences usually begin with 'If' or 'Unless' and are known as conditionals. Another element of conditionals is the use of the verb 'to wish':

I wish I were rich, then I could travel the world.

This peculiar mixing of verb forms occurs in the **present subjunctive**. The present subjunctive expresses suggestions, requirements, requests, or demands. For example:

The doctor ordered that I drink at least two litres of water a day.

'I drink' is in the present tense. The reason for this is that the present subjunctive always uses the base form of the verb (the infinitive). Subjunctive structures in the present (that doesn't yet exist!) typically use verbs like 'ask', 'insist', 'urge', 'require', 'demand', 'recommend', and 'suggest'.

The issue is that this time-bending approach to grammar, the attempt to express what might have been and what may yet still come to pass, is expressed in prosaic forms in everyday English. The *Guardian* newspaper writer David Marsh in his wonderful books on English grammar cites the subjunctive as a dying form that nonetheless has its merits (see Recommendations For Further Reading). I feel it adds a wistful, almost nostalgic quality of expression in the past form:

I wish I were able to clarify this more in effect. (Subjunctive)

Or

I wish I had explained this better. (Confession)

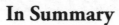

In Summary

The subjunctive describes unreal situations and its particular signature is the use of 'were' (not 'was') for the verb 'to be'. Subjunctive sentences often begin with the conditional 'If' or 'Unless' and the verb 'wish'.

Rule 24

Selecting the Correct Preposition

The Rule: Some words need particular prepositions and choosing the wrong preposition can subtly alter the intended meaning or phrase. There are, for example, lots of exceptions *from* the rules of grammar that many people take exception *to*.

Below is a list of twenty words with their correct prepositions in tow and the contexts in which they should be used:

Adapted *for* – being naturally attuned to a state or circumstances.

Rafael Nadal's style of play is perfectly adapted for clay-court tennis.

Adapted *to* – intentionally having changed due to variable circumstances.

He adapted to living and working in a foreign country.

Agree *to* – a suggestion or proposal.

The President agreed to all the terrorists' demands.

Agree *with* – a statement or idea.

I don't agree with capital punishment.

Change *for* – make an alteration or improvement

I've made a change for the better.

Change *with* – a person or persons or time.

Things change with time.

Change *to* (or ***into***) – physically alter appearance of something or take up a different point of view or circumstance.

I have changed to a different broadband provider.

Confer *on* – bestow something *upon* somebody (or a collective).

I bestow upon you the title of 'King of All of the Belgians'.

Confer *with* – to hold discourse with another person or group of people.

I need to confer with marketing about the new budget proposals.

Confide *to* – to entrust something to somebody else.

The deceased has confided to you all of their worldly possessions.

Convenient *for* – a particular purpose or situation.

This jar is very convenient for storing my toe-nail clippings.

Correspond *with* – a person, as in writing a letter or email.

I have been corresponding with a Russian girl over the internet.

Correspond *to* – something else or other.

These sales figures don't correspond to our projected figures for this month.

Differ *from* – hold a different opinion or point of view.

Where I differ from you is in my attitude to same-sex marriage.

Differ *with* – to be unlike another person.

I differ with my sister on so many levels.

Disappointed *with* or *in* or *by* – something or someone.

I was disappointed by your behaviour on my birthday.

Disappointed *of* – the lack of something or someone.

I was disappointed of the absence of genuinely clever people at the MENSA conference.

Exception *from* – a rule or prescription or situation.

I have an exception from manual labour on account of my feeble health.

Exception *to* – a statement or idea.

I take exception to your argument.

Reconcile *with* – to repair a relationship with a person.

I was finally reconciled to my younger brother at our father's funeral.

Reconcile to – to be resigned to a situation or change.

I was reconciled to the failure of my marriage.

In Summary

As with many technical aspects of grammar, using the wrong preposition with particular words is unlikely to cause any major misunderstandings in common speech because meaning is usually discernible from context. More formal contexts such as reports or academic papers may require greater vigilance however.

Rule 25

Commonly Confused, Misused and Misspelled Words

<u>The Rule:</u> There are pairs of words, often very similar in spelling and pronunciation, which nonetheless have different meanings. Modern spell-checking software does not, as yet, deduce from context so the following list of words provides a guide to common potential malapropisms in speech and writing.

Accept – in agreement with a situation or offer.
Except – to exclude or not include.

Affect – To alter/change.
Effect – The result of a cause.

All together – in the same place, at the same time.
Altogether – as one whole.

Amoral – unconcerned by values.
Immoral – contrary to a moral code.

Appraise – to provide an assessment.
Apprise – to impart information.

Assent – to give permission.
Ascent – to move up or rise.

Bated – to await something in great anticipation: 'with bated breath.'
Abate – to lessen or reduce a hostile element.
Bait – to entice with food; to try to enrage by argument or insult.

Complaisant – eager to please.
Complacent – careless and/or self-satisfied.

Currant – a small dried fruit.
Current – the flow of air, water or electricity; happening at the present time.

Defuse – to calm a situation or disable a bomb.
Diffuse – to distribute over a large space.

Discreet – to avoid attention.
Discrete – separate or individual.

Disinterested – taking up a position of impartiality.
Uninterested – simply not interested at all.

Dual – comprised of two parts.
Duel – one to one contact.

Elicit – to coax a response or reaction.
Illicit – against the rules, prohibited.

Ensure – to make sure/guarantee an action or deed.
Insure – to protect against an eventuality (via compensation).

Fawn – to elicit favour by flattery or servitude; a baby deer.
Faun – mythical beast; half-man, half-goat.

Flaunt – ostentatious display of excess.
Flout – to deliberately break the rules.

Flounder – to have difficulty achieving an aim.
Founder – to fail in an objective.

Forbear – to abstain or desist.
Forebear – ancestors.

Hoard – a collection of objects.
Horde – a group of people.

Imply – to suggest something indirectly.
Infer – to come to a conclusion

Implication – a predicated conclusion drawn by indirect means.
Inference – a conclusion drawn from what is already known to be factually true.

Impassionate – to arouse the passions/strong emotions.
Dispassionate – to be neutral or without prejudice in an assessment or conclusion (not affected by emotions).

Loath – to be reluctant to do something.
Loathe – to hate and despise something or someone.

Meter – a device used for measuring.
Metre – the rhythmic structure of poetry; metric unit of measurement.

Militate – to be a strong force against something.
Mitigate – to lessen the impact of something.

Pour – to cause the flow of a substance.
Pore – to study something intently.

Practice – to adopt an idea or method (put into practice); a legal or medical establishment.
Practise – a repeated physical action in order to gain proficiency in a skill.

Prescribe – medical authorization; issue an order with official authority.

Proscribe – to pronounce something forbidden or illicit.

Stationary – inert, lacking motion.

Stationery – office equipment.

Titillate – to arouse or excite base responses, often sexually.

Titivate – to make something more appealing or attractive.

Tortuous - something of extreme complexity.

Torturous – related to torture, pain and suffering.

In Summary

If you have *got it* don't *flout* it and should someone challenge you to a *dual* be sure to bring a friend along.

When Grammar Goes Wrong

In the world of Google Translate and other online and hand-held translation software applications, it isn't really any surprise that the beguiling structures of English and its innate ability to scramble meaning is getting worse. Here is a selection of public information signs in English from around the world (not all of them are mistranslations from other languages either):

In a cocktail lounge in Norway:
LADIES ARE REQUESTED NOT TO HAVE
CHILDREN IN THE BAR

◆

In a hotel in Acapulco:
THE MANAGER HAS PERSONALLY PASSED ALL
THE WATER SERVED HERE

◆

In a Nairobi restaurant:
CUSTOMERS WHO FIND OUR WAITRESSES
RUDE OUGHT TO SEE THE MANAGER

On a poster in New York:
ARE YOU AN ADULT THAT CANNOT READ? IF
SO, WE CAN HELP

◆

In a city restaurant:
OPEN SEVEN DAYS A WEEK, AND
WEEKENDS TOO

◆

In an Indian maternity ward:
NO CHILDREN ALLOWED

◆

In a Boston cemetery:
PERSONS ARE PROHIBITED FROM PICKING
FLOWERS FROM ANY BUT THEIR OWN GRAVES

◆

A Tokyo hotel's rules and regulations:
GUESTS ARE REQUESTED NOT TO SMOKE OR
DO OTHER DISGUSTING BEHAVIOURS IN BED

◆

On the menu of a Swiss restaurant:
OUR WINES LEAVE YOU NOTHING TO
HOPE FOR

In a Bangkok temple:
IT IS FORBIDDEN TO ENTER A WOMAN EVEN
A FOREIGNER IF DRESSED AS A MAN

◆

In a hotel brochure in Italy:
THIS HOTEL IS RENOWNED FOR ITS PEACE AND
SOLITUDE. IN FACT, CROWDS FROM ALL OVER THE
WORLD FLOCK HERE TO ENJOY ITS SOLITUDE

◆

In the lobby of a Moscow hotel across from a
Russian Orthodox monastery:
YOU ARE WELCOME TO VISIT THE
CEMETERY WHERE FAMOUS RUSSIAN AND
SOVIET COMPOSERS, ARTISTS, AND WRITERS
ARE BURIED DAILY EXCEPT THURSDAY

◆

In an East-African newspaper:
A NEW SWIMMING POOL IS RAPIDLY
TAKING SHAPE SINCE THE CONTRACTORS
HAVE THROWN IN THE BULK OF THEIR
WORKERS

◆

And Finally . . . A Grammarian Walks into a Bar . . .

When grammar pedants have a get-together during the long winter nights it isn't as prosaic an evening as most people might expect. Below are a selection of grammarians' favourite jokes:

A double negative didn't not walk into a bar.

A split infinitive walks into a bar and asks
to first see the menu.

A sentence fragment into a bar.

A pleonasm walked into a pub bar.

A subjunctive mood would walk into a bar,
if they were old enough to drink.

An errant apostrophe walk's into a bar.

———◆———

A conjunctive adverb walked into the bar;
however, they didn't stay.

———◆———

A dangling modifier walks into a bar, after finishing
a drink, the bartender asks it to leave.

———◆———

A dangling preposition found a bar and walked in.

———◆———

Several indefinite pronouns walked into
a bar; a few stayed.

———◆———

A synonym strolls into a pub.

———◆———

The bar was walked into by a passive voice.

———◆———

How Much Do You Know About Grammar? A Quick Quiz

(Answers on page 183 – no cheating!)

1. Which of the following sentences is correct?

    The strawberries that I grow on my allotment taste better than the ones from the supermarket.

    The strawberries which I grew on my allotment tasted better than the ones from the supermarket.

2. Identify the subject pronoun in the following sentence:

    I couldn't understand how she had managed to get there before me.

3. Identify the object pronoun in the following sentence:

    I couldn't understand how she had managed to get there before me.

4. Identify the indirect object pronoun in the following sentence:

   I couldn't understand how she had managed to get there before me.

5. Which of the following sentences is written in the passive voice?

   Melanie took me out to dinner.

   I was taken out to dinner by Melanie.

6. What is the grammatical error in the sentence below:

   I saw two foxes on the way to work.

7. Which is the correct sentence?

   I've been to the gym fewer times this week than last week.

   I've been to the gym less times this week than last week.

8. Which is the correct sentence?

   Who shall we invite to dinner?

   Whom shall we invite to dinner?

9. Which of the following sentences is incorrect?

The killer, who hasn't been named by the police, was arrested last night.

The killer, whom hasn't been named, was arrested last night.

10. Which of the following sentences contains the correct punctuation?

I lost my mobile phone, consequently; I have also lost all of my contact numbers.

I lost my mobile phone; consequently, I have also lost all of my contact numbers.

Quiz Answers

1. The first sentence is correct because 'that' is introducing a defining relative clause. The second sentence requires commas to separate the non-defining clause: ', which I grew on my allotment,'.

2. 'I' is the subject pronoun.

3. 'Me' is the object pronoun.

4. 'She' is the indirect object pronoun.

5. 'I was taken out to dinner by Melanie.' is written in the passive voice.

6. The misplaced modifier – were the foxes on the way to work? It should read: 'On the way to work, I saw two foxes.'

7. Fewer because 'times' is countable.

8. 'Whom' because the people being invited are the object.

9. 'Who' because the killer is the subject.

10. The second sentence is correct as the conjunctive adverb 'consequently' should be preceded by a semicolon and followed by a comma.

Glossary of Basic Grammatical Terms

Adjective – Describes a noun (*lazy, funny*).

Adverb – Describes a verb, adjective or other adverb (*softly, often*).

Antonym – A word with an opposite meaning to another (*clever, stupid*).

Article – Identifies and specifies a noun (*a, an, the*).

Auxiliary Verb – A verb form used in conjunction with a main verb to express additional conditions to an action or state, most typically in the formation of tenses (*have been doing* etc.).

Clause – A group of related words containing a subject and a verb.

Conjunction – A word that connects words, phrases, clauses or sentences (*and, but*).

Interjection – Expresses emotion (*Ah, Ouch!*).

Litotes – Ironic understatement or affirming something by its negative:

e.g. *It was not a good day.*

Modal Verb – An auxiliary verb used to express conditions of modality such as possibility (*might, may*); obligation (*must, will*) or permission (*can, could*).

Noun – A person, place or thing (*table, Paris, David*).

Object – The part of the sentence that the action is being done to.

Participle – A verb form that modifies a noun and often ends in 'ing' or 'ed'. Participles function in a similar manner to adjectives and adverbs:

e.g. *The laughing clown **frightened** the children.*

Phrasal Verb – A verb combined with a preposition in place of a formal verb meaning not always discernible through literal translation:

e.g. *break up, do up, fall out, end up, turn up, work out* . . . etc.

Pleonasm – Placing words of equal or very similar meaning together in a single phrase:

e.g. *extra bonus*

Preposition – A word that comes before a noun or pronoun and expresses a relation to another word or element in the clause (*on, after, for*).

Pronoun – A word that takes the place of a noun (*it, she, he, who, ours*).

Tautology – repeating the same idea within a statement or sentence through the use of unnecessary words.

Subject – The part of a sentence or clause that commonly indicates who or what performs the action (*that is, the agent*).

Synonym – A word with comparable or similar meaning to other words (*little, small*).

Verb – An action or state (*run, eat, be, believe*).

Selected Bibliography

Burchfield, Robert, *The English Language* (Oxford, 1985)

Crystal, David, *Who Cares About English Usage* (Penguin, 2000)

Crystal, David, *The Cambridge Encyclopedia of The English Language* (Cambridge University Press, 2003)

Forsyth, Mark, *The Elements of Eloquence* (Icon Books, 2013)

Foster, Brian, *The Changing English Language* (Macmillan, 1968)

Fowler, H.W., *A Dictionary of Modern English Usage* (Oxford University Press, 1926)

Gwynne, N.M., *Gwynne's Grammar* (Ebury, 2013)

Heffer, Simon, *Strictly English* (Windmill Books, 2010)

Marsh, David, *For Who The Bell Tolls* (Guardian Faber, 2013)

Onions C.T., The Oxford Dictionary of Etymology (OUP, 1966)

Ritchie, Harry, *English For The Natives* (John Murray, 2013)

Swan, Michael, *Practical English Usage* (OUP, 2005)

Index